# Four Paths to Union

Lynne,
May this
book add inspiration
and clarity to your
unfolding! I love you!
Marianne
7/01

## Note from the Author:

In 1981 I assumed the name Mariamne Paulus to express my commitment to take my place publicly as a Light Bearer and as a Wisdom teacher. All books written before the year 2001 have carried my given and married names. This series on the Wisdom Teachings will, however, be published under the name that carries the frequency of the Wisdom tradition and that I use in my teaching.

## Books by Diane Kennedy Pike

*Life As A Waking Dream*

*The Process of Awakening*

*Cosmic Unfoldment*

*The Love Project Way*
*(with Arleen Lorrance)*

*Life Is Victorious! How to Grow through Grief*

*Channeling Love Energy*
*(with Arleen Lorrance)*

*The Wilderness Revolt*
*(with R. Scott Kennedy)*

*Search*

*The Other Side*
*(with James A. Pike)*

# FOUR PATHS to UNION

by

## Mariamne Paulus

 *Teleos Imprint* ~ *Scottsdale, AZ*

*Teleos Imprint*
*Wisdom Books*
Published by LP Publications
7119 E. Shea Blvd.
Suite 109   PMB 418
Scottsdale, AZ 85254-5107

The Teleos Institute World Wide Web site address is
http://www.consciousnesswork.com

Library of Congress Cataloguing-in-Publication Data

Pike,  Diane Kennedy.
  Four paths to union / by Mariamne Paulus.
      p. cm.
   ISBN 0-916192-46-6  (alk. paper)
1.  Mystical union. 2.  Spiritual life.  I.  Title
   BT767.7 .P54  2001
   291.4'4--dc21

                                    2001002830

First Printing, 2001
Printed in the United States of America
*Photo on cover by* Arleen Lorrance

# Teleos Imprint
## Cascade of Angels

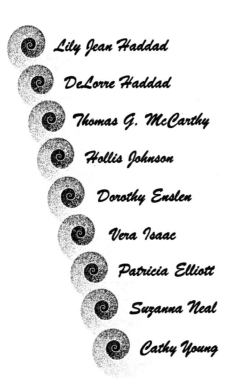

Lily Jean Haddad

DeLorre Haddad

Thomas G. McCarthy

Hollis Johnson

Dorothy Enslen

Vera Isaac

Patricia Elliott

Suzanna Neal

Cathy Young

*Would you like to be included in our cascade of angels?*
*Call 480-471-3082 or e-mail ljh4848@aol.com.*

# AUTHOR'S NOTE

My spiritual quest began when I was very young. I was raised in a small, fundamentalist Methodist Church in the Midwest. My parents were very active in the church and I began attending regularly from the time I was a small child.

I always took religion seriously. As a three-year-old I had my first conscious experience of what I called God. I felt a surrounding and sustaining Presence that so warmed and comforted me that I knew I would always be safe, no matter where I went or what happened to me.

As I grew, I raised many questions about what I was taught in church. I was not comfortable with the idea that all the children in China would be damned to hell for eternity if we didn't get over there to tell them about Jesus so that they could accept him as their savior and be spared such a terrible fate. Nor did I understand how God could be both a loving father and a harsh and punitive judge who would send people to hell. It just didn't make sense to me.

I questioned my parents and other adults in search of answers, but their explanations, when offered, did not satisfy me. Although I tried to figure it out for myself, I could not make sense of much that I had been taught.

I was told that only Jesus could save me from hell,

and I definitely did not want to burn in hell forever, so I did everything I was told to do to get saved. I prayed faithfully every night, I never missed church, I memorized Bible verses, and I went forward at Revival meetings to ask Evangelists to pray for me.

I continued to have experiences of the Presence I had experienced as a child, into my teen years and beyond. When I was twelve I saw and felt light pouring out of my heart to some elderly people for whom our church choir was singing; I took that as an indication I was meant to live a life of service.

Another time, when I was in college, I was enveloped and lifted up into a cloud of unconditional love; I felt that showed me that I was to live in that love. On another occasion in college I felt called to become a teacher and chose my major based on that inner directive.

After each of those experiences I went to a minister to describe what had happened. None of them seemed to know what to say to me. When I awakened to cosmic consciousness at age 28, I knew that I knew all I needed to know. I was one with All; I was both All and Nothing; death had no power over me; all-powerful energy was available to me; I was energy; and human relationships were feeble attempts to experience and know the Union that I had entered.

Yet I was puzzled. My experiences did not conform to the images that had been put before me as a child, and the theology and beliefs I had been taught were not confirmed by what I had seen and felt. I knew I needed to start over on the mental plane with a blank slate and build concepts that were true to what I had come to know directly.

I also wanted to understand how I had come to these profound perceptions and how to live in them as a constant state of consciousness. I was not satisfied to think of these events as gifts of grace. I felt there must be a way to come to such knowing consciously, through the exercise of my own will.

In the terms of this book, I had found my way to the top of the mountain by following the Path of Devotion, but I wanted to work toward Self-Mastery so that I could ascend again with full awareness of what I was doing and how and why.

I left the cocoon of Christianity and found my way to the science of Yoga. There I learned about the Four Paths to Union with the Divine, the All, the One Self, the Absolute Truth. I found it so liberating to understand the Four Pathways that I wanted to share the information about them with others. I began by offering classes and workshops on the Four Pathways to Union. Others responded with enthusiasm to the information, and many requested that I write a book on the subject. It has taken many years, but finally I am making that offering.

My original exposure to the Four Pathways came through **Swami Vivekananda**'s classic series, *Raja Yoga, Karma Yoga, Jnana Yoga* and *Bhakti Yoga*. Thereafter, I found the Paths referred to in many books on the spiritual life, but I remain indebted to Vivekananda for awakening me to them.

I am also grateful to many **students** and participants in classes and workshops in which I, in partnership with Arleen Lorrance, presented the Four Pathways. Their enthusiastic reception of the material encouraged me to make it more widely available, and their persistent requests for the book have urged me on.

Special thanks goes to **Patricia Nerison** for reading my manuscript in its earliest stages, when it was practically incomprehensible, and for making cogent suggestions. Patricia then reread the manuscript in its final draft stage and helped me to refine it with her careful comments.

Thanks also to **Elizabeth Tarpley** for proofreading.

Very special thanks to **Lily Jean Haddad** for her enthusiastic encouragement and marshalling of forces for the publication of this and other books as part of a series on the Wisdom Teachings. Her support in consciousness and in energy has fed my creativity and my inspiration, and her financial generosity and fund-raising has brought *Teleos Imprint Wisdom Books* to life in form.

Finally, I am, as always, indebted to my spiritual partner **Arleen Lorrance** for her ongoing encouragement and support, both in the form of suggestions for the improvement of this manuscript and in the form of confidence that this project could be realized.

I am blessed to be part of a broad spiritual network of individuals walking their chosen Pathways. The companionship we share is a living testimony to much that I present in this text.

> — *Mariamne Paulus*
> *Scottsdale, AZ*
> *February 27, 2001*

# Note to Reader

Many words that would ordinarily not be capitalized are capitalized in this text to call your attention to the fact that they are used with a specialized meaning. For example, path, pathway and way are capitalized whenever they are used to refer to the following of a disciplined approach to a spiritual life. Other words, like real and truth, carry capital letters when they represent perceptions beyond the ordinary realm of objective experience.

I invite you to stretch your mind into new territory throughout this text whenever you see a capital letter on an otherwise ordinary word.

This book is lovingly dedicated to

## Arleen Lorrance

Who walks the Pathway of Action
while supporting me on my own Path
and while providing the most privileged kind
of spiritual companionship and love.
She blesses me with her full presence each day.

And to borrow from another dedication:

*Some give their soul to the Divine,*
*some their life, some their work,*
*some their money.*
*A few consecrate all of themselves*
*And all they have —*
*Soul, life, work, wealth;*
*These are the true children of God.*
*This book is meant for those who aspire for an*
*utter consecration to the Divine.*
*— The Mother*

# TABLE OF CONTENTS

# FOREWORD

The search for an individualized Pathway to Union with the Divine is not widely supported in the West. Judaism and Christianity hold religion to be a personal expression couched in a communal setting. There is little understanding of, or support for, the deeper quest of the individual for the direct experience of knowing, loving, serving, and expressing the Ineffable.

Many in the West label persons who pursue such intimacy with the Divine "mystics" and feel they have withdrawn from reality. Because Western values focus on the secular world, these nonconformists are thought at best to be a little weird and at worst to be heretics or agents of the devil.

Established religions in all cultures have long persecuted nonconformists. For that reason, groups in the West that offer guidance to individuals seeking to go directly to Union with the Divine used to function underground. Their teachings were kept hidden from the authorities and from the masses. For centuries, admittance to Wisdom or Mystery Schools, as they were called, was granted only to those who swore secrecy under penalty of death.

In more recent times secrecy has been preserved in such groups through a consensus opinion that the Wisdom Teachings were beyond the grasp of the average person.[1]

By the end of the nineteenth century, however,

these esoteric (meaning "hidden") teachings began to be offered to a wider public. Recognizing a growing maturity in the group psyche, masters of the Wisdom realized that more and more people would be stumbling on to Pathways and having experiences for which they would have no explanation. There would not be enough teachers available to pass on the Wisdom by word of mouth. So for the first time in many centuries the teachings were committed to writing by such teachers as Alice Bailey, Annie Besant, H.P. Blavatsky, and Rudolf Steiner.

In this increasingly scientific age, the urge to know, and in fact to find out for oneself, is rapidly becoming the fundamental and all-pervasive motivating force. Moreover, Western society holds among its highest values the right of individuals to fulfill their potential. These trends support the growing awareness that a spiritual search outside traditional religious communities is valid.

Within this new context, it seems important to make more widely known four broad Pathways that have long been traveled by those who desire Union with the Divine. To know of them is to be able to find one's way more easily to the growing number of texts and teachers available to the spiritual seeker in this information age.

In this book I offer a broad overview of four universal Pathways for Western journeyers who seek an intimate and personal knowledge of the Ineffable while continuing to live in the secular world. I hope the book will serve to make your individual quest less overwhelming and lonely.

1. Read, for instance, Dion Fortune's comments about preserving the secrecy of what she has been taught in Chapter One of *The Mystical Qabalah,* York Beach, ME: Samuel Weiser, Inc., 2000. She walks a fine line between the old and the new. Also see Vitvan's Introduction to his lesson series on *The Tree of Life,* The School of the Natural Order, P. O. Box 578, Baker, NV 89311, especially pages 8 – 10.

# AN INNER URGE

*Our hearts are restless*
*until they come to rest in thee.*
                    *— St. Augustine*

Deep within each of us there is an inner urge that acts as a kind of homing device. It motivates us to find our ultimate fulfillment in Union with the Divine, the Unspeakable.[1]

Before we become conscious of this spiritual[2] impulse, we experience it in a multitude of guises. We may feel it as a deep desire for union with another person, as a powerful impulse to achieve, as an all-consuming curiosity about life, or as a need to be perfect. Sometimes the urge manifests as fears, such as the fear that we will never belong, that we have nothing to contribute, that there is no meaning to life, or that we will never be good enough. Sometimes it is experienced as restlessness or dissatisfaction. In fact, the universal urge to find Union with the Ultimate gives birth to all human feelings and desires that motivate us to develop our full potential.

This spiritual impulse is revealed in the ordinary activities of life through personality patterns, preferences, interests, and activities. We can easily discern its influence in both individuals and groups when we become familiar with the four broad Pathways that individuals walk when they become *conscious* of their desire for Union.

Unconscious expressions of the Four Pathways are familiar to us as broad human traits. Those whose primary concerns are for the welfare of others and who give generously of their time and energy to meet others' needs and directly improve the lot of individuals reflect the Path of Devotion. All who feel most keenly the urge to make an observable difference in the world at large and who become actively involved in projects or causes designed to effect change resonate with the Pathway of Action. Those who have an insatiable curiosity about life and its meaning and who focus on abstract subjects, thoughts, and studies mirror the Path of Contemplation. And people who are primarily concerned with understanding themselves, with learning how things work through personal experience, and with finding practical applications for that knowledge are echoing the Path of Self-Mastery.

The Pathways are not mutually exclusive. Most of us have some of each motivational force working in us. However, usually one urge is stronger than the others and it results in predominant ways of interacting in the world. We would find it much easier to respect other people and the choices they make in their lives if we understood how the inner spiritual urge is at work in them. Moreover, if we understood that the world religions grew up around the Four Pathways and that cultures arose out of those religious orientations, we would have more tolerance for both cultural and religious differences.

## RELATIONSHIPS
## and the Inner Urge

There are many different approaches to understanding relationships, how they are formed and what makes them work. Many experts address problems of communication within relationships, seeking to discover the causes of barriers and designing strategies to move past them. Very little attention is paid, however, to the fact that a powerful force is at work in all of us that motivates us to make choices and to develop patterns that are fundamental to our differences from others. That the spiritual urge in individuals can be a powerful key to sound relationships and good communication within them is not generally recognized.

Marci and Sam had been married for twenty-four years. They loved each other and had raised three beautiful children together. But there were facets of each that drove the other crazy. For example, Marci was passionate about social issues. She was always involved in one cause or another, pouring her energy into efforts to bring about change. She worked to educate people about pollution and how they could help to clean up the environment. She spent countless hours raising money for housing for the homeless in her community, and with her own hands she had helped to prepare an old house to serve as a shelter for battered women.

When Marci would talk with Sam about these activities, he appeared to take interest, but he never took *action.* Instead, he would probe with questions, seeking to uncover the root causes of the conditions she was concerned about. Inevitably, it seemed to Marci, Sam's incessant questions would take him so far from the actual problem that she lost interest in the discussion. It drove her crazy that Sam asked so many questions, and she would leave the discussion feeling frustrated that Sam seemed incapable of feelings strong enough to arouse him to action.

Sam, on his part, thought that Marci wasted a lot of time and energy trying to change things that would never really change. It seemed to him that the earth had survived for millennia without help from an environmental movement, and he didn't think that recycling a few plastic bottles was really going to affect significantly the changes transpiring in the environment. Although he did not like to see people suffer, he found Marci's efforts to do something to alleviate that suffering almost pathetic. He thought the solution lay in coming to understand the root of violence in human nature and the flaws in our economic system that leave some people unemployed and homeless.

Sam thought that Marci was too impulsive, moving to action before she really understood the underlying causes of the situation. As a result, he felt her actions only tampered with symptoms rather than addressing fundamental issues.

When Marci and Sam attended a workshop in which they learned about the Four Pathways to Union with the Divine, they were ecstatic. At last they could understand their differences! Marci saw that since Sam's primary motivation was to come to know what is True and Real in some fundamental or absolute way, it was understandable that he was always probing, seeking to go deeper. She could see that his questions were not meant to challenge her or her motivations, but rather were his own attempt to find the Truth about the social action movements to which

Marci was devoted. Sam was clearly inclined toward the Path of Contemplation, even though he had no conscious interest in spiritual matters.

When Sam was able to grasp that what mattered most to Marci was to bring about some change in the world around her, he developed new tolerance for her approach. He realized that she had no patience for asking the big questions of life because her focus was on the immediacy of human need. She did not care how or why these situations had come into being. She only wanted to know what *she* could do about them. Marci's principle motivations matched those of the Pathway of Action.

When Marci and Sam understood the urges that were at work in them, they were able to let go of their frustration about their differences and of the feeling that they should have the same response to the world around them. They turned instead to see how they could support each other in consciously walking their individual Paths toward Union.

Margaret was raised in a family of devout Evangelical Christians. In her childhood, she was taken regularly to "tent meetings." Evangelists passed through their small Southern community and held Revivals. For these events, tents were set up at the county fairgrounds, and every evening for a week, people from surrounding communities would gather to hear the firey sermons delivered by the visiting preacher. The congregation would punctuate the preacher's declarations with shouts of "Hallelujah," "Amen," and "Yes, Lord." Often people would forward to give testimony to their own faith and to experiences of being reborn, with tears streaming down their cheeks as they praised God for all His blessings in their lives.

Margaret was embarrassed and offended by the emotionalism of these meetings. She felt people were swept away by the mood of the moment and acted in ways that were undignified and irrational. Moreover, she found many of them to be hypocritical. They professed to have been saved, and yet she knew that they lived in ways that did not conform to the behavior expected of good Christians.

Margaret wanted to understand why she had such an aversion to the religion of her childhood. She wanted to live a good life herself, but she wanted to take responsibility for her choices and not give all the credit to God for what was good in her and all the blame to the devil for her poor choices and honest mistakes. Margaret wanted to use her God-given reason to learn how to live a life of integrity and love.

When Margaret learned about the Four Paths to Union with the Divine, she immediately identified with the Pathway of Self-Mastery. She no longer felt guilty for wanting to understand herself. She affirmed her desire to go back to college and major in psychology even though she was, by then, a middle-aged parent.

Margaret also had a way to appreciate the rest of her family, who were obviously inclined toward the Path of Devotion. Once she understood that the fundamental urge to which they were responding was to express their love and devotion to God, their spontaneous exclamations of praise and thanksgiving were understandable to her. *She* did not feel comfortable with those manners of expression because she was not similarly motivated. It was as simple as that.

That her urge to know and understand herself was also an expression of the urge to Union with the Inexpressible was of great comfort to Margaret, who had long accepted the judgment of her family that she was self-centered rather than God-centered. Now she could see that she was simply expressing her devotion in a different way.

## A SELF-ASSESSMENT

On the pages that follow, you will find a series of descriptions of interests and preferences often shared by people who are inclined to each of the Four Pathways. See which description is *most* characteristic of you so that you can begin to identify your Path. Not all the examples will fit you, but a significant number within one list will speak to you and suggest that you may want to explore this Pathway further. You may discover that one set of descriptors used to be more characteristic of you, but that you have changed your focus now. At the same time, see if you recognize which characteristics are most typical of your loved ones and acquaintances so that you can increase your understanding and acceptance of them and learn how to benefit from their different approaches to life and Union.

### The Path of Devotion

The Path of Devotion is probably your most natural way Home if:

❑ Selfless service to others comes naturally to you.
❑ You love to engage in service projects to aid the poor, the homeless, the handicapped, and others less fortunate than you.

❏ You are devoted to family members and friends who have need of you.

❏ You are a consummate people helper.

❏ You love the feeling of lightening someone's burden or cheering up someone who feels down.

❏ You have felt drawn to, or have chosen as your profession:

▶ social work
▶ medical work
▶ teaching the physically, emotionally or mentally impaired
▶ caring for the elderly
▶ working with the homeless
▶ art therapy
▶ performing arts

❏ You are an artist or a musician and use your art form to express your love of beauty and your gratitude for the privilege of being alive.

❏ You well up with joy in response to the beauty of the world around you.

❏ You wake up in the morning filled with enormous gratitude for the blessing of life itself and all you have received in it.

❏ You find yourself breathing out joy during the day for the smallest delights, like the smile of a child, the perfection of an athlete's body, the contentment of a sleeping cat, the majesty of a towering mountain, a flower that has just opened, or the taste of a succulent piece of fruit just plucked from the tree.

❏ You have been active in a church and enjoy group worship services in which you share the companionship of others as you offer your praise and thanksgiving to God.

❏ You are deep feeling and emotional by nature.

❏ Your heart is easily touched.

❏ You long to know, and to be transformed by, the most comprehensive Love possible.

❏ Your favorite question is **who** can I serve?

## The Path of Action

The Path of Action may be your most natural way Home if:

❏ People call on you when they want someone to undertake a project and see it through to the end.

❏ Your principle response to problems is "Why doesn't somebody *do* something?"

❏ You feel impatient and restless when people complain about the way things are in their life or in the world but do not take action to change anything.

❏ You respond to people's statements of their beliefs by asking what difference those convictions make in the way they live their lives.

❏ You are drawn to social action movements.

❏ You are an artist or a musician and use your art form to motivate others to take action in the world around them.

❏ You often volunteer your time and skills in organizations whose purpose is to serve the local, regional, or global community.

❏ You watch for ways to take action on issues such as world peace, world hunger, human rights, human freedom, and human justice.

❏ You have felt drawn to, or have chosen, a profession such as

> ❯ law
> ❯ politics
> ❯ mediation
> ❯ fund-raising
> ❯ community action work
> ❯ philanthropy
> ❯ construction
> ❯ architecture
> ❯ service in the Peace Corps
> ❯ teaching
> ❯ the arts

❏ You are an active member of your neighborhood and community, organizing and participating in efforts to make life better for succeeding generations.

❏ You don't care how much money you earn so long as your job enables you to make a difference in the world.

❏ You see the Ineffable in the world around you, both in natural beauty and in the lives of individuals who, through their direct action, have changed the course of history.

❏ You have been attracted to religious congregations and secular organizations that emphasize social action.

❏ You express your deep feelings through what you do.

❏ You enjoy the feeling of camaraderie when people are working together on a project that will impact their neighborhood, community, state, nation, or even the world.

❏ Your favorite question is **what** can be done?

## The Path of Contemplation

The Path of Contemplation is probably your most natural way Home if:

❏ You find most conversations banal and superficial.

❏ You prefer to be alone so that you can reflect on important matters and engage in stimulating intellectual pursuits, through books and your own writing.

❏ You have always asked many questions in your efforts to understand things that most people take for granted or consider recondite.

❏ You are intellectual by nature.

❏ You are fascinated by data that expands the horizons of your understanding so that you see a bigger picture of how things are in the universe.

❏ You engage authorities on any subject in discussions of the fundamental assumptions underlying their approach.

❑ You are drawn to the theoretical and the abstract,
   loving the feeling of stretching your mind to its limits.
❑ You are strongly attracted to fields such as
   ▶ philosophy
   ▶ logic
   ▶ theology
   ▶ theoretical science
   ▶ theoretical mathematics
   ▶ general semantics
   ▶ teaching (usually in higher education)
❑ You enjoy vigorous debates with other knowledgeable
   people.
❑ You hope to develop, or have developed, a personal
   philosophy that addresses all the great questions
   about life.
❑ You spend long hours in deep contemplation of
   inquiries into matters that interest or distress you.
❑ You long to know what is True and Real in some
   fundamental or absolute way.
❑ You are as interested in questions as you are in
   answers, if not more.
❑ You find it difficult to belong to most religious or
   fraternal organizations because the members seem to
   accept what the leaders say without question and fail
   to use their own minds to evaluate group assumptions
   or actions.
❑ You find references to "God" too simplistic to interest
   you.
❑ Your favorite question is **why**.


## The Path of Self-Mastery

The Path of Self-Mastery is probably your most
natural way Home if:
   ❑ You find yourself the most fascinating subject of all
      and love to read books or to try approaches that take
      you deeper into yourself, giving you suggestions for

how to improve your life in one area or another.

❏ You love to go to workshops and classes that teach you ways to improve your life.

❏ You have gone for counseling or psychotherapy.

❏ You enjoy going with friends or your partner to workshops where you can practice interpersonal skills together.

❏ You find it difficult to accept anything as true until you come to know it through your personal experience.

❏ You are an artist or a musician and use your art form to perfect your own technique in order to express what is deep within you.

❏ When you learn a new skill, you seek to master the technique, whether physical, emotional, mental, or spiritual.

❏ You enjoy teaching others how to do things.

❏ You find yourself suggesting to others what they can do to heal themselves, to improve a relationship, to relieve stress, or to tame their minds, based on your own experience.

❏ You are an advocate for education on all levels.

❏ You have been drawn to the fields of:
> teaching
> psychotherapy
> counseling
> coaching
> mediation
> laboratory sciences
> applied sciences (technology)
> the arts

❏ Psychic healers, psychics, hypnotists, magicians, shamans, and medicine men fascinate you because of their abilities to work with powers beyond the ordinary.

❏ You long to know the Ultimate Power directly, through your own personal experience, and you want to understand *how* you can arrive at that experience.

❏ You have had psychic or spiritual experiences that you

long to understand so that you can repeat or sustain them.
❏ Your favorite question is **how.**

Did you find one of these descriptions more characteristic of you than the other three? If so, you may want to read about that Pathway first. If not, you may find that your interest is awakened by the more detailed descriptions you will find in the chapters that follow.

And perhaps you discovered that each list seemed to describe loved ones and friends. If so, then you already have a taste for the benefit of understanding the Four Paths to Union. Learning to recognize the motivating forces that are at work in ourselves and in others helps us to respect our differences.

## CHILDREN
## and the Inner Urge

Children who seem different from other children often mystify adults. For example, earlier I referred to Sam as one whose motivations seem to reflect the Pathway of Contemplation. His parents, who did not share his inclinations, became concerned about him even before he went to kindergarten. As a toddler, he spent hours by himself playing with his favorite toys. As he grew older, he taught himself to read. He did not seem to enjoy the company of children his age, but he would engage with adults who were willing to respond to his probing questions: Why is the sky blue? Where does water come from? How can birds fly? Why did Uncle Carl die? Where did he go? Where does God live? Can flowers hear?

Sam's parents were afraid he would never learn to make friends and would be a social outcast. They imagined that he would be miserable in school. When they enrolled him in kindergarten, they expressed their concern to his teacher. The teacher used all her skills to try to draw Sam out and help him make friends, but with little success. However, she quickly discovered that Sam was eager to learn; he outpaced his classmates in every area except social skills.

It might have been helpful if Sam's parents and teachers had recognized that even as a child, Sam was responding to an inner urge to focus on those things that captured his imagination. He was simply devoting himself to what was of most interest to him. In doing so, he was developing his mental capacities of focus and concentration. With guidance and encouragement, Sam could have developed his unique gifts at a much younger age than he did.

I am reminded that both Albert Einstein and Thomas Edison did poorly in school. Neither was very socially adept. Yet their preference for inner reflection and concentration enabled them to make invaluable contributions to humanity. Sociability is not the ultimate test for a life well lived, especially when spiritual urges are taken into account. Sam's urge to concentrate and reflect deeply on his interests suggested that he would step onto the Pathway of Contemplation one day. His parents and teachers would have benefited from some understanding of the nature of that Path.

Sam may have chosen Marci as his mate, whether consciously or unconsciously, to bring more sociability into his life and to balance his tendency to be a loner.

Other children's patterns reveal different inner urges. Melissa's parents worried about her, not because she was unsociable but because she seemed to have no fear whatsoever. She began to bring stray and wounded animals home with her when she was tiny. As she grew older, she began to reach out to children who were taunted by their peers or who were handicapped in some way. She befriended them in every way she could. She sometimes brought a street person home for dinner. She never asked whether an animal or human *could* be cared for. She assumed they *would* be, and she took the first steps in that direction. She had no awareness of practical matters like the cost of care or the danger of inviting a stranger into her home.

Melissa's parents were concerned that she lacked boundaries. They tried to teach her that there are bad people in the world and that you can get hurt. They told her that she (and they) did not have the resources to care for every stray animal and person. They felt she would never be able to live in the world as it is.

If Melissa's parents had understood the Path of Devotion, they would have recognized that Melissa was exemplifying the spirit of selfless service that characterizes that Way to Union. They might have been able to support and guide her with greater understanding and wisdom.

Then there was Brian. His parents were concerned that he was too much of a perfectionist and too introspective. He was, they felt, overly sensitive to criticism. Whenever someone suggested he had done something wrong, he was deeply wounded. He would then try doubly hard to correct his mistake. He would spend long hours practicing any new skill until he could do it "right." Moreover, it seemed he took everything personally. He was quick to apologize to other children when they got hurt, even if he was not responsible for what had happened, as if it was his fault for not preventing the mishap. If his parents scolded him for something he did, he would go to his room and spend hours thinking it over. Then he would emerge to apologize and promise to do better.

If Brian's parents had understood the Four Pathways, they might have recognized Brian's urge as belonging to one who aspires to Self-Mastery. Then they might have guided and directed his urge, teaching him self-love and patience to go along with his desire to master whatever he undertook.

And what about Kelly? She earned the name Little Miss Fixit very early in her childhood. She was the oldest of four children and she hovered over the little ones, looking for ways she could be helpful. Her parents scolded her for doing everything *for* her brother and sisters. They were afraid the younger children would not have an opportunity to learn. But Kelly seemed to have little patience for their learning process; she preferred to do things herself.

Kelly also took charge of things in the neighborhood, telling the other children what they could do and how to do it. The children on the block found her bossy and a know-it-all, but they also knew they could count on her when they needed someone to organize their play or to get them out of a jam. Kelly always seemed to know what to do.

When Kelly started school, she immediately became a "teacher's helper." She loved to be given tasks to do. She took her responsibilities seriously and was proud of her accomplishments at the end of each task. Her teachers loved her but many of her classmates resented her. Kelly's parents worried that she would grow up to be a meddlesome adult. If Kelly's parents and teachers had understood that the Pathway of Action was natural for her, they might have helped her.

Kelly was responding to an inner urge to make things happen in the world around her. She needed to learn how to harness that urge and put it to good use without intruding in the lives of others. That lesson cost Kelly a lot of heartache through the years. Her motivation was good, but she often overstepped her boundaries.

In addition to providing food, clothing and shelter for their offspring, most parents attempt to inculcate values and habits that will enable their children to be successful in society. They would serve an even higher purpose if they encouraged their children to follow the inner spiritual urge that is fundamental to a meaningful and fulfilling life. To do that, they need to be able to identify the most common expressions of that urge, to affirm the child's natural inclinations, and to give guidance to and express appreciation for preferences different from their own.

## FRIENDS and PARTNERS

It is not just that parents and teachers would be able to give better support and guidance to children if they understood how inner spiritual urges show up in personality patterns. Any of us can more wisely support friends and partners as well when we are knowledgeable about the Four Pathways. Personality differences, such as Marci and Sam's mentioned above, often prove vexing if we do not have a larger context within which to understand them.

It will be of value to you to read about the Four Pathways, not only in the hope that you will be able to identify your own, but also so that you can better understand other people. Perhaps you have already experienced Union with the Divine and know your oneness within, with All, and with the Absolute. Understanding different approaches to the experience you have had will expand your circle of companionship along the Way.

---

1. Insofar as possible, I use words other than "God" to refer to the Ultimate with which we long to unite, because "God" often has only emotional content for people and thus does not aid verbal communication. Other words may be equally ineffective, but I hope they will stretch your mind and imagination in the direction of the all-encompassing, indefinable, original source of all of which we are conscious. However, when describing the Path of Devotion, I use the term "God" because it is so widely used by those who walk that Pathway.

2. By spiritual, I mean an urge that comes from the "spirit," that aspect of humans that is impersonal, transcends the space/time continuum, and has faculties of consciousness beyond the ordinary human faculties.

# THE METAPHOR:
## FOUR PATHS TO UNION

*We may reach the same goal by different Paths.*
*— Vivekananda*

Teachers of the Wisdom have used a simple metaphor for hundreds of years to illustrate the nature of a spiritual Pathway. They speak of a mountain that represents ultimate Truth, or what most people refer to as "God." There are many ways to ascend that mountain. At the base of the mountain the various Pathways seem very far apart. Aspirants give different reasons for climbing and their longings seem quite different one from the other. However, as they climb they discover that their Paths merge, for there is only one Truth.

When Union is realized at the summit, aspirants find they are one with each other as well as with the ultimate Truth. That Union is experienced as the fulfillment of the meaning of human existence. The term "spiritual Pathway" takes its meaning from this metaphor.

A spiritual Path is the method you choose to facilitate your ascent of the mountain. When people reach the summit, they describe their experience of

Union in many ways. It has been described as the development of a refined character with a highly evolved moral nature, as intellectual illumination, as a realization of the Self, as salvation, as awareness of one's immortality, as wholeness, absolute peace, Truth, Knowledge, Wisdom, joy, and/or bliss.

We might say that there are as many Pathways to Union with the Divine as there are persons who have come to know the unnameable One. But there are certain major approaches to any summit. Although climbers may take shortcuts or sidetracks or invent new ascents or drops, still they will be traversing, let us say, the east, west, north or south face of the mountain.

## The Southern Face

On the southern face of the metaphorical mountain, the sun is the warmest, the rocks are relatively smooth, and the view of the peak is clear. Those who climb the southern face value being in the presence of that peak for the entire journey and are not concerned about how long it takes to reach the summit.

These aspirants feel awe that they are blessed just to climb in the presence of the summit. Their hearts are full of joy and gratitude as they ascend. They often sing as they climb, and they feel privileged to be able to help anyone they find along the way who has stumbled or fallen or grown weary and given up.

These climbers are on *the Path of Devotion*.

## The Western Face

Pathways on the western face of the mountain wind through heavy forests in which there are wild animals, abundant plant life, and many other climbers camping out, organizing side excursions, providing entertainment, and selling supplies. It is almost impossible to measure whether one is making any progress on the western face because there are very few places where one can see the peak. But these aspirants love the climb.

They love the natural environment through which they travel and the other creatures that inhabit it. They find innumerable ways to be of service to the other human beings they encounter along the way. They join teams to clear the paths and create campgrounds and way stations. They organize rescue operations and clean-up crews. Sometimes they feel there may be no summit and that Truth, or the Divine, will be found only in the other climbers and in the natural environment they traverse.

These climbers are on *the Path of Action*.

## The Northern Face

The northern face of the metaphorical mountain is barren, the rocks are sharp, and there is little warmth from the sun. Those who climb the northern face are hardy individuals who find the clean, cold air exhilarating. They tend to be loners, for not many people are drawn to this ascent. The summit is not visible from the northern face and thus it is not self-evident that it even exists.

These climbers are motivated by a paradoxical passion for Truth. On the one hand, they are confident there is a peak and that it can be reached. They love the challenge of using their minds to find their way without clear outer direction. On the other hand, each time they believe that they have found the quickest ascent or that they have seen the summit, another rise appears on the horizon. No truth ever seems complete or final to them. Their passion does not subside, but their confidence that there is anything ultimate may waver. Yet they press on, testing their paradoxical faith and doubt at every turn.

These climbers are on *the Path of Contemplation*.

## The Eastern Face

Those who climb the eastern face of the mountain are motivated by a deep urge to know their own capacity to meet this challenge. They work hard to prepare themselves for the climb with exercise and proper nutrition. They examine their motivations to be certain they want to make this effort. They study maps of the route they have chosen.

They rise early to make the ascent in the light of the rising sun. They find the way rigorous, with many hazardous crevices to cross. When obstacles appear along the way, these climbers use them to strengthen their determination to complete the climb and to hone their skills and capacities. They thrill to the challenge on all levels — physical, emotional, and mental — and value the experience of the climb even if they never reach the summit.

These climbers are on *the Path of Self-Mastery*.

You may be new to the idea of stepping onto a spiritual Path, or you may have already begun your ascent of the mountain. In either case, ask yourself, "What is my deepest longing?" Breathe into your belly as you ask the question. Take time to feel what you long for in your deepest center and put it into words. Feeling your longing and holding your own words in your awareness, read the chapters that follow. Do you recognize yourself in any of these traditional formulations of the Four Pathways?

Such self-reflection, which is important to aspirants walking all Four Pathways, will help you to identify the Path to which you are *most* drawn at this stage of your life. You might become aware that you had a stronger drawing to a different Path at an earlier time in your life. Or you may discover at some time in the future that you wish to cross over to another Pathway. Nevertheless, identifying your predominant urges *now* will help you to gain clarity regarding both your past and your future.

Read the presentation of each of the Pathways in a spirit of inquiry and self-reflection. If you feel you know which Path is "yours," start with that chapter. Keep checking with your intuition throughout to see what fits for you and what doesn't.

Then read about the other three Pathways. By comparison and contrast, see if you still feel as strongly about the one you chose first.

If you do not know which motivational urge is strongest in you, then read through the chapters in any order you choose. But remember to read them while breathing into your solar plexus (belly) to see what *feels* right to you. What feels familiar? What seems to fit the way you know yourself internally? I hope you will identify your Path to Union with God (Devotion), with All that Is (Action), with Truth (Contemplation), or with Self (Self-Mastery). Your Pathway will make it possible for you to cooperate with that fundamental urge that is pressuring you from within to become all you are capable of being.

A secondary benefit from reading about all Four

Paths is that you will be able to understand other people at a deeper level. You will develop more tolerance for their differences when you recognize that they may be responding to an inner spiritual urge. And if you have already experienced Union yourself, you will find it easier to understand why not everyone wants to climb the mountain the way you did.

You will also perceive the world religions differently, recognizing the contributions they are making to the whole and appreciating the importance of their differences. Knowledge of the fundamental motivating forces makes it easier to comprehend cultural predispositions. The peoples of the world could more easily live in peace together if differences were honored and all groups stretched to meet each other halfway between the Paths.

For example, many Westerners who travel in India are put off by the poverty they see there. They criticize the Indians for being lazy and failing to improve their physical conditions. If those same travelers understood that India has spent thousands of years under the powerful influence of the Path of Devotion, they might see things differently. The Indians fill their days with acts of devotion. They are full of love and generosity. They go out of their way to express kindness to others, not for any material benefit but as an expression of their Love for the Divine. Let me give two examples.

A friend of mine went to India alone, on a spiritual pilgrimage. It was his intention and desire to visit several ashrams (retreats) of teachers whose writings he had studied. He did not realize how profound the cultural shock would be for him. When he arrived in Mumbai (Bombay), he was suddenly filled with fear.

He had taken a bus into the center of the city, but he needed to find a place to stay and to book his travel to the ashrams. He did not know whom to trust.

The traffic, both vehicular and pedestrian, was overwhelming. As he stood on the street, bewildered and frightened, a young man about his age approached him. In perfect English, he asked if he could help. Fred told him his dilemma. The young man immediately said, "You will come and stay the night with my family. Tomorrow we will arrange for your travel."

The young man took Fred home. His family welcomed him with unconditional Love. As Fred told them of his desire to visit the ashrams, the mother said, "You cannot travel alone. My son will accompany you." Fred protested, but the family insisted. The son would take leave from his job and go with Fred. "As long as you are in our country, you are our guest," the mother said.

To Fred's surprise, there was no way to dissuade them. They were not a wealthy family. They lived in a small apartment and were obviously dependent on their son for part of the family's financial support. Nevertheless, for the next several weeks the son was Fred's constant companion, translating for him, helping him to make arrangements, keeping him company.

From the Western perspective, there was no way this gift could ever be returned. From the Indian view, there was nothing to repay. The Indians acted out of Love for Fred because of their Love for the Divine, and they considered it *their* privilege and blessing to serve Fred in that way.

A Westerner might say, "But what about the guy's job? What about the income he lost? What about the cost to the family?" Those values, which have developed in the West under the influence of the Pathway of Action, paled in comparison with the opportunity to express unconditional Love and to be of service to a human being in need.

I could tell you many similar stories. But let me offer this one. Another friend of mine was in India on one of her frequent trips. While walking along a dirt path toward the hostel where she was staying, she suddenly felt faint. Unable to stop the process, she fell on the ground unconscious. When she awoke she was in a humble hut resting on a thin mat on a dirt floor. Hovering over her she saw the concerned faces of strangers. A young man said, "I found you unconscious along the path and carried you home. I was afraid you would come to harm there, or even die."

Only the young man spoke English, but the entire family ministered to Marie until she was well enough to walk back to her room. The young man accompanied her to make sure she arrived safely, and for the next several days he checked back with her to make sure she was all right.

This gesture of kindness and caring was not an exception, it is the rule in India where people accept the responsibility to serve even strangers in Love. The people may be materially poor, but they are rich in an abundance of Love.

Cultural values and ways of living often reflect the influence of the predominant spiritual Pathways. Once you know the characteristics of the Four Paths you will be able to identify their influence in your own culture and in others'.

The mountain of the incomprehensible Whole stands before you. If your urge to penetrate that vast mystery is strong enough, you will find a way to cooperate consciously with it. To do so is to step onto a Path in quest of knowledge through Union with ultimate Truth, the All, the one Self, or God.

# THE PATH
# OF DEVOTION
## A LIFE of
## LOVING SERVICE

*Love the Lord your God
with all your heart, with all
your soul, and with all your mind.
And love your neighbor as yourself.*
— *Matthew 22:34-40*

The Path of Devotion will serve you if you are predisposed to selfless service, if you spontaneously adore the Infinite and are full of an all-consuming desire to love God and to be enveloped in God's Love. This may be your Path if you are motivated by very deep feelings, and you lift those feelings, often spontaneously, into your Heart where the force of Love dissolves all barriers between self, others and the Infinite. If you live in an inner atmosphere of joy, thanksgiving and praise to such an extent that it sometimes annoys friends and family when they feel discouraged, ungrateful, and resentful about aspects of their lives, then this Pathway may well be yours.

The Path of Devotion has permeated Western civilization through the influence of Christianity.

Christians come together for worship at least once a week, expressing through song and prayer their praise and thanksgiving to God. They are devoted to Jesus as the embodiment of God's Love, and many give countless hours each week to various forms of service as a natural expression of their Love of God. These practices are typical for those who walk this Pathway.

If you have felt at home in Christianity, Hinduism, Sufism, or Hassidism as a religion, there is a strong possibility that the Path of Devotion will serve you well as you undertake your individual journey Home. If you have felt restless within one of those religions, wishing the congregation were more dedicated to social action, you will want to look deeper into the Pathway of Action. If you have been impatient with Christianity, Hinduism, Sufism or Hassidism for not making room for your intellect, telling you to "have faith" rather than inviting you to raise your sincere questions born of a desire to understand, you may be better suited to the Path of Contemplation. And if one of those religions has not helped you to understand yourself and has not given you step-by-step guidance in developing your faith and your spiritual life, then perhaps you will be happier with the Pathway of Self-Mastery.

If you think this is probably *not* your Pathway, you may want to turn now to another chapter. If you do that, I would encourage you to come back later to this chapter so that you can better understand others. Since Christianity predominates in our Western culture, it is helpful to understand the nature of the Devotional Pathway that gives Christianity its form and texture. You will undoubtedly have persons in your life who are, by nature, inclined to this Pathway or who have chosen it for their passage to Union with the Divine. Reading this chapter will help you to understand and love them.

In addition, you may well find that you feel an affinity with some of the elements of this Pathway, but not with all. You may still want to follow some of the suggestions below to supplement the disciplines of the Path you choose and to enhance the quality of your life in general terms.

## FIRST STEPS ON THE PATH

If you consciously choose to find Union with the Divine on the Pathway of Devotion, how do you take your first steps? Walking a spiritual Path is not about declaring your belief in something, nor even about understanding the nature of the Path. It is about actually doing something about it.

Here are some suggestions for first steps you can take.

### <u>Step One:</u>

Each morning as you awaken, breathe into the joy of being alive. As you experience the Life Force flowing through you, quickening your pulse and arousing your muscles to a day of new self-expression, awaken gratitude in your heart for the gift of life. Breathe into your heart center and breathe out gratitude over and over again. Let a smile of happiness brighten your face. *Feel* the wonder of life and the privilege of enjoying it in this body and this personality with this set of life circumstances at this time in history.

Find a way to offer your thanks that feels right to

you. It may be through ejaculations of "Thank you father/mother God." It may be by addressing the angels that surround and guide you, or a spiritual master, or the spiritual hierarchy. Perhaps you simply address the whole universe with exclamations of joy and thanksgiving. Whatever form fits for you, express your thanks in a way that helps you to feel your connection to the larger Whole of which you are a part.

Practice this way of beginning your day until it is as natural as opening your eyes when you awaken.

### **Step Two:**

Throughout each day, pay attention to all your blessings. When other drivers cut you off in traffic and give you dirty looks as though you were at fault, be grateful that you are not pressured or unhappy and so can bless them on their way. When a new stack of laundry has replaced the one you just finished putting away, offer thanks that you and your family can afford so many clothes. When others are complaining that your plane is late reaching its destination, thank God that you all arrived safely. When it rains on a day when you planned to play golf, feel grateful for four or five unexpected free hours that you can use in some other creative way. Find something to be grateful about in everything that happens throughout each day.

As I was writing these words, conscious of the blessing of a quiet, uninterrupted hour in a lovely hotel room, the housekeeper came in to make up my bed and bring me clean towels. I noticed that she was humming a lovely melody while she worked in the bathroom. When she came in to make the bed, I asked Ruby how many rooms she had to make up each day. She said fifteen. "That's a lot of beds to make," I commented. Her response was a perfect example of the practice I am suggesting here. "Yes, it is," she remarked, "and I'm so grateful to have a job."

"How long have you worked here?" I pursued. "Fifteen years," she said. As we talked further I mentioned that I had heard that the new owner was going to make big changes. "I just hope he has a place for us," she said. "I am grateful for the benefits I get and for a month's vacation each year." Her face was radiant as she spoke. Ruby is a definite candidate for walking the Devotional Pathway!

Sometimes the challenge to be grateful seems enormous. When my husband died and I was suffering great pain at the loss of him, I reminded myself over and over again that if I had not loved him as much as I did, I would not feel so much pain. That always opened my heart to the privilege of having known him, loved him, and shared my life with him. I was eventually able to be grateful for the pain that reminded me of that.

When a dear friend of mine found out her abdomen was riddled with cancer, she, who walked the Pathway of Devotion, immediately embraced the cancer with gratitude. She told me, "Isn't it wonderful that I have time to prepare for my death? That is the blessing of cancer; it gives you ample warning." Rather than spending her time and energy on radiation and chemotherapy, she chose to "show people how to die."

Look for opportunities to express your gratitude actively. When people render services for you, thank them. Do not dismiss what they have given you with the thought, "Well, that's their job." When loved ones do what is expected of them around the house, tell them how much you appreciate them. Praise them when they do the job especially well. Never take anything for granted; use each occasion to express thanks.

When you have an opportunity to render a service, whether at home or at work, express your gratitude for the chance either to the one you are privileged to serve or to God from whom all life flows.

Practice this step of counting your blessings and expressing your thanks for them throughout each day until doing so is second nature.

### Step Three:

Each evening, just before you go to sleep, do a gentle review of the day. Awaken gratitude in your heart for each gift that came into your life, in the form of persons, experiences, events, opportunities, challenges, responsibilities, etc. Breathe out gratitude for each thing, including those that were painful or difficult. And as you drift off to sleep, rest into a Heart full of thanks for the gift of another day fully lived.

### Step Four:

Awaken in yourself a fervent desire to be an embodiment of Love. Read devotional literature and the stories of God-inspired individuals. There are countless books and magazines available that will inspire you with thoughts, stories, poetry and prayers. Such literature is spiritual nourishment for the one taking first steps on the Pathway of Devotion. Don't let a day go by without partaking of something inspirational, either spoken or written.

A friend of mine lived alone. She had fully incorporated these first steps of the Path of Devotion into each day. After her morning quiet time in which she offered prayers for her loved ones and gratitude for her life, she sat down to her breakfast alone. She used that time to read her devotional magazines. In that way she nourished body and soul at the same time.

You will find the time that fits best in your daily schedule. It should be a time when you can give undivided attention to what you read or listen to, even if for only five or ten minutes.

## Step Five:

Express your joy through song. Nothing caresses your Heart like your own voice lifted in song. Sing or chant your way through each day. If you have no words to use, then hum your melodies of praise and thanksgiving. If you can't carry a tune, then learn to tone, which is a way of letting the voice soar that does not require words or a tune.[1] Find a way to experience the thrill of expressing joy and praise and thanksgiving as song.

If you *can* carry a tune, find a choral group to join. There is nothing more uplifting or gratifying that singing in harmony with a whole group. It will do your Heart good.

Listening to fine music will also inspire and uplift you, but it can never take the place of using your own voice.

## Step Six:

Practice embodying unconditional Love with everyone you contact throughout each day. The Love Principles [see Appendix One] will help you to make your Love expressions both genuine and practical. Whenever you find it difficult to Love someone, refer to the Love Principles to see which one you are not applying. You will find it relatively easy to identify what attitude or value you need to change in order to let Love flow through you freely and without obstruction.

Practice opening your heart to persons you dislike or disagree with. Receive into your heart individuals who are so different from you that you can't identify with them at all, and those who make you feel uncomfortable because they are deformed or handicapped or behave in ways you find bizarre. In other words, open your heart wide enough to embrace everyone.

It is not enough to feel pity or compassion. Your challenge is to Love. When I was breaking down the barriers around my Heart, I challenged myself to look life in the face and see it for what it was. Life came to me through individuals. One day I stepped out of a supermarket and ran right into a man who was so drunk that he had vomited all over his clothes. His hair was matted with filth. He was slobbering and mumbling and stumbling and falling.

I knew this was a supreme opportunity for me to practice. I found a place to sit down close enough to smell the man. As I watched him, I breathed into my Heart. I took in the stench and the ugliness and opened my Heart to it all. I breathed out Love to this man, visualizing a great stream of energy pouring out of my chest toward him. After some time I began to *feel* Love for him. I kept breathing into the Love until my mind stopped speaking to me about how awful he looked and smelled and sounded. Then I simply Loved him, for a long time. I began to see him as one of God's precious beings, and I knew that if I did not see his beauty the limitation was in me, not in him.

On another occasion I was walking down the

street in a large city. A homeless man came up to me to beg for money. My impulse was to turn away, so I disciplined myself to stop in front of him and look him in the face. "This is God," I reminded myself. I listened to him. I looked in his eyes to contact the Being. He suddenly said, "What I *really* need is a hug." For a split second I thought of my dress and his filthy jacket. Then I remembered that I wanted more than anything to be able to Love unconditionally. So I took an enormous breath, opened my Heart and my arms, and embraced the man right there on the street. To my surprise, the man stepped back, smiled at me, and said, "Thank you." Then he turned and walked away.

I tackled every situation that was difficult for me. I held an obese man more than twice my size and weight while he was having an epileptic seizure so that he would not injure his head. I looked into the eyes of a group of young men on a city street when I inadvertently walked onto their turf and they began to call out to me with suggestive and obscene remarks. I greeted them with my Heart open and a simple "Good morning." Then I made a conscious choice, having purchased the newspaper I had gone out for, to pass by them again. As my eyes met theirs and I looked deeper to meet them Being to Being, they returned my greeting with "Good morning again." And I smiled.

My most difficult challenge was to learn to Love a politician who had come to represent for me everything I was opposed to in the national and international arena. I had grown to hate him. To transform that hate took real concentration. I used his every television appearance and every newspaper article about him to practice breathing through my Heart to embrace him in Love. It took me years to bring about the transformation, but by the time of his death I was more than twenty years into the practice. I felt only compassion toward him, and was able to bless him on his way.

I could tell you countless stories, but you will have your own. Think back to times when you moved past your preferences or opinions in order to express Love for someone, whether a neighbor, a difficult relative, a coworker, or a relative stranger. My point is that you will want to practice Love all the time, wherever you are, with everyone you meet. And that Love must be sincere. Only you can know if your Heart is open and the Love is flowing freely.

You practice unconditional Love because you know that this is the way God Loves, and your ultimate goal is to completely merge with God. Therefore, you seek to become *like* God by learning to Love as God Loves. As you Love human beings, remind yourself that you are Loving God through them. Let your Love for the Divine grow within you until you can begin to feel it like a fire in your heart.

### Step Seven:

Practice active forgiveness of all those in your life, both past and present, who have hurt you, disappointed you, failed you, or done you wrong in some way. You cannot Love unconditionally if in your Heart you harbor feelings of ill will against certain individuals. To the extent you are unable to forgive anyone, you are unable to Love all others. The energy that you withhold from others is *for giving* to them in Love.

When I was practicing this step, I used to sit each morning in quiet and stillness and ask, "Whom do I need to forgive today?" Then I would wait until someone came into my consciousness. Sometimes I could not remember immediately what I held against the one who came to mind. But if I waited and asked, I always remembered. Sometimes the incidents dated back many years and I was shocked to discover that I was still harboring that energy in my Heart that was meant *for giving* in Love to the other.

I continued this practice for months. Sometimes I reached out to the individual and actually expressed my forgiveness, usually by writing a letter. I don't recall if I ever received an acknowledgment of any of those letters of forgiveness. But the acknowledgment was not the point. The essential thing was to release from within myself the energy that I had been withholding.

Often I did not contact the individual. Some had already died. I had not had any contact with others for many years and did not know how to reach them. Others had never known of the ill will I harbored toward them. In this latter category were many politicians and personalities on the national and world stage who had impacted the world in ways I had considered unforgivable. I looked within myself to find ways to forgive and release. Sometimes it took me days or weeks of my quiet time in the morning to find the way to let go of my resentment or hard feelings.

You may discover that you have not forgiven *yourself* for some of your past behavior, or even, perhaps, for being who you are. To practice forgiveness of self is perhaps the most difficult of all. It is sometimes helpful to imagine that you are opening the gift of Love and forgiveness that God has already given to and for you. As you allow yourself to experience this forgiveness, to take it in on the feeling level, your unconditional Love of self will begin to grow within you.

This is not an exercise to be done in a superficial way. Unless you do it genuinely, you will not truly forgive. Undertake this practice with the understanding that God's Love, that life-giving energy, flows out to all living beings. If you want to Love God, and to Love as God Loves, find it within yourself to Love all humans, one by one, including yourself.

### Step Eight:

Find ways to be of service. On the one hand, make everything you do all day long an act of service, especially those things you are expected to do because they are your responsibility or a part of your job. On my first visit to India, I heard people say again and again, when I thanked them for their service, "It is my duty." This phrase was always accompanied by a smile and a bow, and I could see that these devout Hindus, whose religion teaches them the basics of the Path of Devotion, were conscious that in serving me they were serving God. Their duty brought them joy.

I learned a lot from their example. I began to recognize the blessing every time I had the opportunity to serve another human being with my actions. I learned that in serving others I was serving God.

On the other hand, it is important to be on the alert for opportunities to serve in unexpected ways. One morning I was playing tennis. A man skated by on his roller blades. Suddenly he tripped on the uneven sidewalk and went flying. He cracked his forehead open on the cement.

I immediately ran out the gate of the tennis court and knelt beside him. I urged him to lie still because his head was bleeding and asked him if he minded if I helped stop the flow. He said he did not. Then I used what I knew about healing energy to stop the bleeding, telling him all the while what I was doing and what I observed about his wound. When the bleeding had stopped, I helped him get to his feet. When he felt steady enough to skate to his car, I watched him on his way and urged him to have his head looked at because he needed stitches.

I never saw this man again, but to this day when I think of him my heart wells up with joy to have been able to serve him in his time of need. To act in that way requires letting go the boundaries of "it's none of my business." You must act instantly, knowing that each opportunity to be of service is a unique occasion to express unconditional Love.

When I was a child, we used to sing a song in Sunday School that said, "God has no hands but my hands to do His works of Love." I often think of that tune that so fully expressed the attitude of one who walks the Pathway of Devotion.

If you feel ready to walk the Path of Devotion, be happy. Love life. Delight in your circumstances. Be grateful for all you have and for every experience. And find joy in each opportunity to be of service.

If, after a few weeks or months of practicing these first steps, you find your heart singing and you feel "I am headed Home," then you may indeed have found your Pathway.

## MAKING A COMMITMENT

If you feel confident that you belong on the Pathway of Devotion, you will want to make a commitment within yourself to do all that you can do to make steady progress on this Path. The commitment will be made in the solitude of your own Heart. It will be a commitment to yourself to remain true to what is right for you. It will be made with the understanding that this is a solitary journey. You alone are responsible for your choice, your commitment, your progress, your failures, and your ultimate success.

You do not step onto a spiritual Pathway in order to please someone else or to gain recognition for your commitment. You do it because your innermost being demands it. You cannot do anything else and remain true to yourself.

Once you are certain you have found the Pathway that will take you to Union with the Divine, you will begin to deepen the practices you began as your first steps.

## Embody Love

To pursue Union with the Divine on this Path, you must, to use Jesus' words, "hunger and thirst after righteousness." You can only know God by becoming *like* God, by becoming Love embodied.

Those who walk the Pathway of Devotion are convinced that no one has ever seen or known God except through other humans. Therefore, you may seek out someone who is the very embodiment of God, an Incarnation, as described on page 191. If you find such a being, you will probably follow, serve, worship and adore that one. Jesus, for instance, told his followers, "Anyone who has seen me has seen the Father" (John 14:9b) and "I am in the Father, and the Father in me" (John 14:11). As one who seeks to know God in his personal, or embodied, aspect, you will find your way made clearer if you focus on one in whom you see God revealed in His true nature: that of Love.

Both Christianity and Hinduism are world religions with devotional orientations, and in their practices can be found many of the disciplines followed by those who walk this Pathway. Among the Muslims, a large movement called Sufism represents those who walk the Way of Love. In Judaism, it is the Hassidim who have brought forth this spirit of joyful celebration of life and given it form.

If you devote yourself to the spiritual life, however, you will transcend the practices of any given religion and adopt a single-minded and whole-hearted focus that fulfills your own urge to know God through Love. If you should choose Jesus as the object of your devotion, or Krishna, or Sai Baba, or some other Incarnation of the Divine, you will seek to walk in his steps, following his example while loving God in and through all you do.

We were fortunate in the twentieth century to have had an outstanding exemplar of this Pathway living among us in Calcutta, India. Mother Teresa was a Roman Catholic nun, but her sense of self was universal. She said, "In my work, I belong to the whole world. But in my heart, I belong to Christ." She was a living expression of the Devotional Pathway. She made a commitment to devote herself wholly to God and to the service of her neighbors. Eventually that commitment deepened and she renounced everything to follow Christ into the slums, to serve the poorest of the poor.

In the unfolding of Mother Teresa's work in Calcutta, and from there, throughout the world, we have a visible expression of the steps one takes who walks the Way of Love. It is helpful to have such an outstanding contemporary example of the Pathway of Devotion, because the commitment required is very personal and all encompassing. One can be devoted to a supreme example, such as Jesus or Krishna, but it is extremely inspiring to know that even in our time it is possible to embody God's Love fully and unconditionally.

Of course not everyone on the Devotional Pathway serves the poorest of the poor, Thomas Kelly, a devout Quaker who walked the Devotional Path, said that from the holy center of the adoration and Love of God deep within, come the commissions of life. "Our fellowship with God issues in world-concern" (120). In other words, if you Love God, you will serve humanity in some way.

You will want to dwell within your Heart for long hours when you are prepared to commit yourself to this Pathway until the desire to know God, and to Love God, and to serve people as an expression of your Love of God, completely envelopes you. Then continue to dwell in the sanctuary of your own Heart to hear *how* you can best serve as you walk the Way of Love.

If you are drawn to an exemplar of this Pathway who inspires your devotion, all the better. Because your challenge is to *embody* Love, to focus on someone who does that  is very helpful.

If you choose the Path of Devotion to gain Union with the Divine, you may be known among your friends as a devotee, and those who do not trust deep feelings may accuse you of belonging to a cult, for they will not understand your commitment to an exemplar of a life lived in Love. Others may think of you as a mystic, for Love will be your only means and your only end, and your most passionate desire will be to know the blissful state of the ecstatic Love-Union with God. Your friends may not understand the fervor with which you approach life. The very powerful and personal feelings that motivate you may seem strange to them.

But your heart will sing, for you will know that you have found the way that suits your nature as you move toward Union with God. You will adopt this as your life purpose: to Love God with all my heart, and to Love my neighbor as God Loves me. This commitment will carry you forward with unfaltering fervor during the remaining phases of the ascent toward Union.

## Purify Your Personality

Once you are fully committed to Love God and to serve others as an expression of that Love, you will want to purify your personality so that Love fills your whole being. It takes great strength of character to walk the Devotional Path without sinking into an excess of emotionalism that becomes self-serving. Therefore, it is important to purify your body, your feelings, and your thoughts.

All the practices you began as first steps on this Pathway will continue to serve you as you progress along the Way. You will want to intensify your life of prayer. Most people who choose the Path of Devotion are sustained by powerful images, myths, symbols and rituals. Familiar examples from the lives of Christian mystics are the symbol of the Crucified Christ, statues or images of saints, the story of Jesus' life (held as a myth representing the journey of the soul in its awakening), and the ritual of the Mass, or Holy Communion. All the great devotional religions have such symbols and myths. Individuals who step on the Path of Devotion continue to find inspiration from the myths that the religions preserve, the symbols and images that represent embodiments of Love, and the rituals that awaken their desire to know God.

Within Christianity the story of Jesus' life is a compelling myth about giving one's life in unconditional Love and service to God. The life of Krishna who danced for joy in his Love of God provides a powerful myth for devotees within Hinduism. You may find that your Heart hungers to hear such stories and to be elevated by them.[2]

## Select Images of the Divine

You will want to have symbols of the way you have chosen as visible reminders of your life of Devotion. Symbols make it easier to remember your commitment to Love. They can be as simple as a photograph of persons who are living examples of the embodiment of Love. For example, I have friends who surround themselves with pictures of Sai Baba, an Indian man who is revered as an embodiment of God's Love. Another friend had on his puja table (altar) a large picture of Ananda Moyma, an Indian woman who radiated God's Love. Or, you may want to have statues to represent Jesus or Krishna or other incarnations of the Divine, or of saints or mystics who have walked this Pathway. These symbols will help you to hone the focus of your thoughts and feelings.

The image of Divine Love, which is an ideal chosen by one walking this Path, is held constantly in mind and heart. It serves to inspire acts of Love as well as being the object of expressions of Love and Devotion. Mother Teresa held Jesus as her ideal. She said the following about her life and work:

> We serve Jesus in the poor. We nurse him, feed him, clothe him, visit him, comfort him in the poor, the abandoned, the sick, the orphans, the dying. All we do — our prayers, our work, our suffering — is for Jesus. Our life has no other reason or motivation.
>
> This is a point many people do not understand. I serve Jesus twenty-four hours a day. Whatever I do is for him. And he gives me strength. I love him in the poor and the poor in him. But always the Lord comes first. . . . It is for him we work, to him we devote ourselves. He gives us the strength to carry on this life and to do so with happiness.
>
> Without him we could not do what we do. We certainly could not continue doing it for a whole lifetime. One year, two years, perhaps; but not during a whole life, without thought of reward, without expectation of anything good except to suffer with him who loved us so much that he gave his life for us. Without Jesus our life would be meaningless, incomprehensible. Jesus explains our life. (25-26)

Such devotion is beyond the comprehension of many of us but it is the very core motivation for one walking this Pathway. It is passionately emotional, and yet it requires the distillation of all emotions into one holy expression of Love for the Divine.

## Say Name Prayers

The repetition of prayers using names that represent embodiments of God is very helpful to one walking the Devotional Pathway. Common examples of such prayers are, "Thank you, Jesus," or "Hare [which means *praise*] Krishna," or "Hail, Mary," or "Sai Baba, Sai Ram." Repeated continuously throughout the day, such name prayers help to transmute the natural desire for human love and companionship into an all-consuming longing for the Divine. To remember God through a rhythmic, repetitive invocation of God's name also focuses consciousness on God and places the devotee in His presence. The chanting of OM, Father/Mother/God, Ram, or Allah are examples of such invocations. "To become absorbed in recitation is to forget about worldly attachments and rest in God" (Esposito 111).

## Perform Rituals

If you do not belong to a group with whom you can participate in rituals, you will want to develop some of your own. It is helpful to set up a small altar in your home where you can place your symbols of Divine Love. Some Christians call these shrines, and in Hindu homes they are called puja tables. They are a visible focus for your worship of the Divine.

Establish daily rituals as acts of Devotion. It is important to involve all of your senses in these daily rituals. You may want to light candles and place fresh flowers to enliven your visual involvement. Incense will awaken your sense of smell. Prayers said aloud, hymns that you sing, or chants you intone will enable you to hear your Devotion expressed. Some form of communion in which you ingest food or drink that represents Divine Love will involve your sense of taste. Physical movement will awaken kinesthetically the sense of touch. Common expressions are kneeling, bowing, gesturing with the hands (as in folding the hands in prayer, making the sign of the cross, or placing the palms of the hands together at the heart), or using prayer beads or rosaries.

The purpose of these myths, symbols and rituals is to feed, nurture and motivate you as you progress on the Path. They heighten your Devotion and keep your feelings and thoughts focused so that you live constantly in the presence of the Divine and are filled with Divine Love. This requires the development of strength in body, mind and will so as to maintain a harmonious balance without any excesses.

## Other Practices

Many devotees purify their bodies through **dietary practices**. There may come a time will you will be motivated to practice regular fasting, which will help reduce your physical cravings for food. Fasting may also give you greater control over your sexual desires and help you to direct your creative energies into various expressions of service. You may also give up meat-eating for a time, or permanently, as a way of cleansing your emotions and gaining greater jurisdiction over them.

Other devotees place great attention on the exercise of **compassion and nonviolence**, feeling that they are natural components of the embodiment of unconditional Love. You will have already spent time forgiving those against whom you held resentments or hard feelings, and loving those who might once have been difficult for you to Love, including yourself. Now you may be moved to awaken the capacity to see God in all creatures, not just in humans. The practice of nonviolence is one way of acknowledging the inherent beauty and value of all sentient beings.

For most devotees, the use of music, chanting, songs and hymns is an important part of the discipline of offering praise and thanksgiving to God. In the Sufi tradition, the combination of **music and dance** proved especially popular among the people as a quick way to become intoxicated on God, to experience deep emotional feelings of Love for God and to feel His closeness. The most famous example of the use of dance among the Sufis is that of the whirling dervishes. They practice staying utterly centered and conscious of the inner Presence as they twirl. Their movements follow ritualistic patterns. The group embodies the Sufi understanding of the universe as individuals lose their sense of separation and experience Oneness. A similar practice of dancing among Christian mystics caused one group to be called Shakers.

## SPIRITUAL DIRECTION

When you have chosen your ideal, you will have a source of instruction regarding the walking of your Path. Here are some examples of the kind of direction you might receive. Krishna instructed his disciple with these words:

> The first requisites for spiritual life are these: doing no injury; being truthful, honest, nonattached, modest; abstaining from wealth; maintaining faith in an after-life;

practicing continence, silence, patience, forgiveness, fearlessness, physical and mental purity, austerity, self-reliance, hospitality; chanting the name of the Lord; performing sacrifices; surrendering the self to me; making pilgrimages; working for the good of others; and serving only the teacher . . . These, my friend, if rightly followed, bring great spiritual unfoldment. (Prabhavananda 142)

Mother Teresa guided her Missionaries of Charity with similar steps:

A young girl wishing to join our society must meet the four conditions that are required to be a Missionary of Charity. She must be healthy of mind and body. She must have ability to learn. She must have plenty of common sense and a cheerful disposition. . . . We try to teach them, from the very beginning, to pray while working, doing it for Jesus and doing it to Jesus. (16)

Mother Teresa also stressed that the sisters should learn both inner and outer silence, humility, charity, and joy. "The best way to show our gratitude to God and the people is to accept everything with joy. A joyful heart is the normal result of a heart burning with love" (37).

## PERFECT LOVE

When your personality is completely purified and your dedication to God is total, then all forms and rituals will fall away. Images, temples, churches, religions, sects, countries and nationalities will be superseded, and nothing will remain to bind you to a worldly orientation. You will direct everything to God and serve always the highest Ideal of Perfect Love.

Perfect Love has three aspects:

## 1. No Bargaining

Love is given because God is worthy of Love, and for no other reason. The Lover gives freely, expecting nothing in return. Love is selfless, and without reward. When Love is expressed to and for others, it is an overflow of this selfless Love of God. The Love is given for itself, not for any result.

This kind of service is different from that rendered by the disciple following the Pathway of Action, which is intended to bring about change in the world. The disciple on the Path of Devotion has no interest in transforming the shape of society or institutions. The only desire is to Love God. As Mother Teresa expressed it:

> If there are people who feel that God wants them to change the structure of society, that is something between them and their God. We must serve him in whatever way we are called. I am called to help the individual, to love each poor person, not to deal with institutions. God has not called me to be successful. He called me to be faithful. (97-98)

Motivated to express Love for God by loving individual human beings, Mother Teresa made no apology for her work in the world. She said:

> I know that there are thousands and thousands of poor, but I think of only one at a time. Jesus was only one and I take Jesus at his word. He has said, "You did it to me . . ." My sisters, the brothers, and I, we take one person, one individual person, at a time. You can save only one at a time. We can love only one at a time. (20)

This is Love offered for its own sake, not to gain anything in return and not to see any particular results in the world. Although when you walk this Pathway you long for Union with God with an intense fervor, you are nevertheless content every step along the way just to Love God. The loving is enough. Not even Union with God is held as part of a bargain.

## 2. No Fear

Perfect Love casts out all fear, Jesus said, and when you walk the Path of Devotion you will come to know through experience the truth of this statement. You will have no fear of failure, no fear of loss, no fear even of suffering, and certainly no fear of punishment. You will live in the unfailing assurance of God's Love and Presence. Not even descriptions of hell inspire fear in a devotee, because you know God is also there.

I remember hearing Hannah Hurnard, a British woman who walked the Path of Devotion with great fervor, affirm that she was not afraid of hell. She said she would want to go there because she knew Jesus would be there, ministering to all those suffering souls. Her face shown with Light as she affirmed that she would want to be there beside him, serving in Love.

Here are Mother Teresa's affirmations of this supreme confidence born of Love:

> God always provides. He will always provide. Though we have no income, no salary, no grants, no church maintenance, yet we have never had to send anybody away because we didn't have . . . I have never been in need . . . I need nothing for myself. (51)

If there is no alternative to persecution and if that is the only way that Christ wants to come among his people, by radiating his Love for them through my actions, I would stay to serve them, but I wouldn't give up my faith. I would be ready to give my life, but not my faith. (195)

John, the Beloved Disciple of Jesus, expressed another version of the same confidence:

There is no room for fear in love; perfect love banishes fear. For fear brings with it the pains of judgment, and anyone who is afraid has not attained to love in its perfection. (I John 4:17b-18)

And Rabia al-Adawiyya, the great Sufi saint, said:

O my Lord, if I worship Thee from fear of Hell, burn me in hell, and if I worship Thee in hope of Paradise, exclude me thence, but if I worship Thee for Thine own sake, then withhold not from me Thine Eternal Beauty. (Smith 30)

By walking the Path of Devotion, you will come to know what it is to live with no fear.

### 3. No Rival

When you choose an ideal of embodied Love, whether that ideal is reflected in a religious figure like Jesus or Sai Baba or someone in your personal acquaintance, you will hold that ideal above all else that is of value in your life. Nothing else can rival it. You will be totally devoted to that ideal. Mother Teresa chose Jesus as the embodiment of her highest ideal. She said about him:

I am nothing. He is all. I do nothing of my own. He does it. I have loved Jesus with my whole heart, with my whole being. I have given him all, even my sins, and he has espoused me to himself in tenderness and love. Now and for life I am the spouse of my crucified spouse. (195-196)

This is the kind of total Devotion you will come to know and to experience as you walk your Path.

As you walk this Pathway of Love and Devotion, then, you will begin with a peaceful love and a quiet, inner desire to know God. As the fire in your heart grows, you will become a servant, motivated solely by Love. Through that service you will discover God as friend and playmate, as parent and as child, and finally as spouse.

For Mother Teresa, Jesus became the focus of her Love for God. She said, "To me Jesus is my God. Jesus is my Spouse. Jesus is my Life. Jesus is my only Love. Jesus is my All in all. Jesus is my Everything" (107). But not everyone focuses on a person. Laurel Keyes, who was one of my mentors, walked this Pathway. She said that she had no other purpose in her life than to serve and share the Love that overflowed her days. But her ideal became an invisible Beloved within. In her spiritual autobiography *Sundial: I Count the Sunny Hours,* she wrote this poem about her ideal:

Who is this, my Beloved, you ask?
It is His voice that calls me
To awaken with the dawn.
You would hear only bird voices
But I know it is my Beloved calling.

It is for Him that I cook and clean
And bake and mend.
For His pleasure that I put
Each blossom in its place
To make a composition of fragrance and grace.
Each act I do is my offering of love
To my Beloved.

He touches me.
A thousand ways He has of touching me,
Thrilling me with each.
A gentle breeze lifts the hair above my cheek
And a kiss,
So gentle, so tender –
I turn to see
 Surely He is there!
A leaf glints golden in the light
A star glows to brightness in the night –
That is His passing – here, there – everywhere.

His gifts to me?
Those are many.
Each flower turning its opened heart to sun
Is one he caused to blossom just for me,
He flings a rainbow across the sky
Or sprinkles frost in sunlight
To make the world enchanting
Just for me.
There is never a wish that He were nearer me
To share a joy unfolding
To think of Him is to have Him
Beside me.
His voice whispers in the pines
Or in the lull of waves along the beach.

I have only to look – He is there.
Only to call, and hear His answer.

I am alone – only when I forget Him.
Of children we have many,
Every one who turns to us in need is ours.
In serving them, we serve our own,
In watching them grow, we watch our own,
In guiding them, together
We see the fruition — of the seeds of our love.


All this –
And yet, I surrender myself completely,
Holding back not one shadow of a part of me,
The nearness of His presence is overpowering me.
Sense of time and space, pride and fear,
Of duty, service, gain or loss
Vanish –
I let them go
As I would gladly let my life go
Into His keeping
And ask for nothing more.

I must burst with the miracle of Love
Which fills me –

I am lost
　　　In oneness
　　　　　　With Him – My Beloved –

There is no beginning, no ending.
There is no He,
No I,
There is one,
A divine ecstasy of a Nothing which is Everything
And, forever.

You must find your own Beloved –
Then you will know. (417-421)

This is the spirit and attitude of one who walks the Pathway of Devotion.

## THE DANGERS

On every spiritual Pathway there are certain dangers about which the disciple needs to be warned. The Path of Devotion works with the emotions, fueling them and then lifting them into the Heart. For this reason, it is sometimes seen as the easiest Path, because we humans are very emotional. It is natural for us to feel deeply about things. To walk this Pathway, all we need to do is to take that natural inclination and direct it to God.

However, for the same reason, this is the most difficult Pathway. Emotions are very difficult to direct. They are changeable and often seem unmanageable. Moreover, we are drawn to love many persons and things, and to hate many others. Loving God with *all* one's heart and soul and mind is a daunting task.

Those who become disciples on this Pathway must pay special attention to the need to purify the body and personality because of how easy it is to fall into excesses. There are many devotees who focus on Love of the Divine only to find that they fall into bed with their teacher or guru. Divine Love gets channeled into sexual expression instead of human love being elevated to Love of the Divine. Unless you know your physical appetites well and have learned to control them, it is easy for the passion of Divine Love to be misdirected into excesses of sex, food, or drink.

If the emotions have not been purified, the disciple can fall into another kind of excess. If preferences, likes and dislikes remain alive in the solar plexus, the fervor of Divine Love may evoke a matching distrust and hatred of any who are perceived as "enemies of the faith." Love for the ideal can result in hatred of all else. On the personal level, this can lead to animosities based on differences in perception of what is good and beautiful. Vitriolic diatribes in the name of one's ideal are commonplace around the world. These passions lead to fanaticism, holy wars, and the persecution of unbelievers with which history is replete. Cruel actions may be justified as necessary to defend "the faith" and may even be called "God's will."

If the mind has not been purified, the fervor of Divine Love can lead to a fanatical conviction that "my way is the one and only way." The small leap from "this is my way to which I am whole-heartedly committed" to "this is the one and only way" can cause the disciple to become narrow-minded, unforgiving, and harshly judgmental of those who do not walk "the" way. The attitude can be sanctimonious, righteous, and rigid.

If the body is not cared for and kept in balance, a devotee can actually do physical violence to himself in the name of Love. St. Francis, for example, was so transported by his Love of God that he practiced a harsh asceticism in relation to his body. He was physically ill for the last several years of his life and died at age forty-four.

If there is an imbalance in the personality, the Devotional Pathway can also lead to emotional or mental illness. A lot of force is released through the fervor, and the personality must be strong enough to tolerate it.

Even when the disciple on the Path of Devotion

strives for balance, she can have difficulty keeping her feet on the ground. The powerful energy of Devotion can transport you into such ecstatic states that it is difficult to function in the world as most people know it.

For all these reasons disciples who walk this way must purify body and personality and develop qualities to support the will in its Devotion to God alone. With this focus it is believed that one single moment of the madness of extreme Love of God can bring eternal freedom. In the East, respect is paid to those who have gone mad in their Love of God. They wander the streets in a blissful state and are supported by the charity of others. But in the West, disciples must return from such moments of Divine madness to take responsibility for their own lives. That is the challenge of this Pathway in the West.

## SUMMARY

How, then, shall we characterize the Path of Devotion in summary?

It is a simple Pathway that works with human desires and impulses and gradually transforms them in the fire of a Divine Love. As you walk on this Pathway you will be embodying the two great commandments given in the Old Testament and reiterated by Jesus:

> *Love the Lord your God with all your heart, with all your soul, with all your mind.* (Matt. 22:37)[3]

You will do this as you:

✦ purify the desires of your heart so that you Love only God even as you see Him expressed through and reflected by humans and other living things;

✦ purify your personality so that only qualities that enhance and support Love remain, qualities such as truthfulness, sincerity, selflessness, forgiveness, generosity, and kindness. In the words of Saint Paul:

> Love is patient; love is kind and envies no one. Love is never boastful, nor conceited, nor rude; never selfish, not quick to take offence. Love keeps no score of wrongs; does not gloat over other men's sins, but delights in the truth. There is nothing love cannot face; there is no limit to its faith, its hope, and its endurance. (I Cor.13:4-7)

✦ purify your mind so that you are cheerful and hopeful, seeing the good and believing that all is possible in Love, and strengthening the mind so that you can use it to discipline the senses and the passions.

✦ purify the body through abstinence, fasting and the choice of life-giving foods, leaving it strong and healthy and responsive to the impulse of Love moving within it.

### *Love your neighbor as yourself.* (Matt. 22:39)[4]

This commandment points to the devotee's life of service. The importance of loving other persons as a way of manifesting your Love of God is expressed beautifully in this passage from the New Testament:

> Dear friends, let us love one another, because love is from God. Everyone who loves is a child of God and knows God, but the unloving know nothing of God. For God is love . . . he who dwells in love is dwelling in God, and God in Him. . . . But if a man says, "I love God," while hating his brother, he is a liar. If he does not love the brother whom he has seen, it cannot be that he loves God whom he has not seen. And indeed this command comes

to us from Christ himself: that he who loves God must also love his brother. (I John 4: 7-9a, 16b, 20-21)

And to Love your neighbor *as* yourself, you must Love yourself, for it is not possible to Love others un-conditionally unless you also Love yourself.

When you walk this Pathway, Love and Devotion are the means and the goal, the instrument and that which is to be attained. Love is valued above all.

In practicing the embodiment of Love with total dedication and devotion, you walk the Pathway of Love and Service and discover the bliss of the Union in which Love, the Lover, and the Beloved are One.

---

1. See *Toning,* by Laurel Elizabeth Keyes, Marina del Rey, CA: DeVorss & Co., 1973; *The Roar of Silence,* by Don G. Campbell, Wheaton: The Theosophical Publishing House, 1989; and *Healing Sounds: The Power of Harmonics,* by Jonathan Goldman, Rockport, MA: Element Books, 1992.

2. You will find these stories compiled in the Holy Books, like the Bible and the Bhagavad Gita. You can have access to many of these great myths in one volume if you consult *The Bible of the World,* Edited by Robert O. Ballou, New York: The Viking Press, 1939.

3. Also, Deut. 6:5.

4. Also Deuteronomy, throughout.

**Works Cited**
The New English Bible.
Esposito, John L. *Islam: The Straight Path.* New York/Oxford: Oxford University Press, 1988.
Keyes, Laurel Elizabeth. *Sundial: I Count the Sunny Hours.* Denver: Gentle Living Publications, 1979.
Kelly, Thomas R. *A Testament of Devotion.* New York: Harper and Brothers, 1941.

Prabhavananda, Swami. *The Spiritual Heritage of India.*
Hollywood: Vedanta Press, 1979.

Smith, Margaret. *Rabia The Mystic and Her Fellow-Saints in
Islam.* Cambridge: Cambridge University Press, 1928.

Teresa, Mother, of Calcutta. *My Life for the Poor.* Edited by Jose
Luis Bonzalez-Balado and Janet N. Playfoot. San Francisco:
Harper & Row, 1985.

# THE PATH OF ACTION
## MAKING a DIFFERENCE in the WORLD

We must be the change we want to see
in the world.
*— Mahatma Gandhi*

People who walk this Pathway are highly principled humanitarians and change agents. They are very responsive to their conscience and are eager to do what is right. They love what they see as good for the world, and they rejoice when they see a way to multiply that good.

The Path of Action will serve you if you are willing to work hard for what you consider to be a good cause, if your love and concern motivate you to take immediate action, and if getting the job done is sufficient reward for you. This may be your Path if you get restless listening to what you consider to be idle talk with no action to back it up, or if you consider it restful to shift from one kind of activity to another instead of just resting. If friends and family accuse you of not being able to sit still or of being a workaholic, this Pathway may well be yours.

The Path of Action has permeated our Western civilization primarily through the influence and legacy of Judaism. The Jews were called to worship One God by keeping a set of commandments as a people. As a community they were, from the beginning, faithful to laws that gave structure to their life and interactions. Their religion was practiced primarily in the home where faithfulness to God was made evident by certain practices that reminded them of their relationship to God. Among Jews, *how* you live and *what you do* is far more important than what you believe.

Because Christianity emerged out of Judaism, respect for the law and a feeling of responsibility to the larger community has been a strong theme for Christians, too. Both religions have built schools and hospitals, established community action programs, and undertaken projects to help the poor, the homeless, and the powerless. These activities and concerns are typical for those who walk the Pathway of Action.

If you have felt at home in Judaism, or in Christian congregations that place special emphasis on social action, or in churches like the Society of Friends or the Unitarian Universalists, or in Muslim communities whose focus is on justice and right relationships, there is a strong possibility that the Path of Action will serve you well as you undertake your individual journey Home.

If you have felt restless in Judaism or activist Christian groups, feeling there was too much love of action and not enough love of God, then you may be better suited to the kind of service that characterizes the Path of Devotion. If you have felt that social activists do not take time to examine the deeper questions, such as why these conditions exist in the world and whether they can ever in fact be eradicated, then you may find greater resonance with the Path of Contemplation. And if you observe activists and see that their attitudes and lack of human relations skills often work against them, then perhaps you will find the Pathway of Self-Mastery meets your needs.

If you think this is probably *not* your Pathway, you may want to turn now to another chapter. If you do that, I would encourage you to come back to this chapter later so that you can better understand others. Ours is a culture firmly based in pragmatism. We believe in getting things done. If anything, we are overly active. Much of our Western culture rests on the tradition of Judaic law, and the values of the Judeo-Christian religions give shape to much of our communal life. Therefore, it will be very helpful to understand the nature of the Pathway of Action. You will have many people in your life who are, by nature, inclined to this Pathway or who have chosen it for their passage to Union with the Divine. Reading this chapter will help you to understand and love them.

## FIRST STEPS ON THE PATH

You do not need to believe in any doctrine to walk the Pathway of Action. In fact, you may not believe in anything transcendent. You may not know what your soul is or engage in any kind of spiritual conversation. But you *will* need to be conscious of *why* you do what you do in every situation if you wish to use this Path to find Union.

In the East, this Pathway is called Karma Yoga. The word Karma is derived from the Sanskrit work

*Kri,* meaning "to do." Therefore, all action is Karma. Technically, the word also means the *effects* of actions, which is how most Westerners use the word. However, when applied to a spiritual Pathway, the word Karma has the meaning of *work.* Everything you do, whether physical or mental, is Karma, and leaves a mark on you and on the world around you. Therefore, *you need to begin to think of everything you do as your life work.*

Through your actions you build character, for you become what you do. And because the effects of your actions go out toward others, you also affect what others become. And you help develop the nature of the groups to which you belong. This is the law of cause and effect, which is often called the law of Karma.

If you choose to move toward Union with the Divine on this Pathway, how will you take your first conscious steps? Since action is your preference, you will be ready to begin at once, but activity alone is not sufficient. If you choose this as your spiritual Pathway, you need to examine your intentions, your purpose.

## Step One

Read the biographies and writings of the great humanitarians of the twentieth century, such as Albert Schweitzer, Mohandas Gandhi, Martin Luther King, Jr., Clara Barton, Eleanor Roosevelt, Nelson Mandela, Cesar Chavez, Dorothy Day, and Susan B. Anthony. Look for what motivated them in their activities. What were their highest ideals, their life purposes and supportive objectives, the qualities and skills that characterized their personalities? What signs of moral integrity and high-mindedness do you find? Let yourself be challenged and inspired by their examples.

### Step Two

Ask yourself, "What effect do I want to have on the world around me, and on the people whose lives I touch?"

Many people respond to this question by saying that they want to leave the world a little better than they found it. But you need to know what will make it better, according to your ideals. Do you want people to feel more secure, to know they are loved, to have more education, to know how to live in peace with other people, to take responsibility for the welfare of others, to make their highest contribution to the world around them, to be free, to be healthy? Identify as specifically as you can what you consider to be the highest good for the world around you.

Albert Schweitzer (1875-1965) was a great philosopher, physician and humanitarian in the twentieth century. He was committed from the time he was young to serve humanity through both thought and action. Before he was thirty he was a respected writer on theology, an accomplished organist, and an authority on the life and work of Johann Sebastian Bach. At thirty he returned to University studies to become a medical doctor, and in 1913 he established a hospital on the edge of the forest at Lamborene, Gabon (then in French Equatorial Africa). In his first year, he served 2000 patients in his hospital.

However, he was not satisfied until he was able to name the *principle* by which he was living his life.

When the phrase "reverence for life" came to him, he felt he could finally articulate his highest ethical value. He believed that humans could reconcile the drives of altruism and egoism by requiring a respect for the lives of all other beings and by demanding the highest development of the individual's resources. This was not only his personal philosophy, but this was the imprint he wanted to leave on the world around him. In 1952 he was awarded the Nobel Peace Prize in recognition of his humanitarian efforts, but it was not until many years later that reverence for life began to permeate Western thought as a real possibility through the Ecology movement.

Like Schweitzer, you may find it easier to *be* the change you want to see happen in the world than to put it into words. But once you are able to identify what you want for others, you will have laid the foundation for your life objectives.

## Step Three

Ask yourself, "What kind of person do I need to be to have such an effect?" This question arises out of an understanding that the effects of your actions are determined more by the quality of your character than by the nature of the work itself.

During the 1960's and 1970's, I was active in the anti-Viet Nam War movement. My deep longing was for world peace. People who were supportive of the war used to ask me, "How do you know peace is possible?" For a long time I thought the question was ridiculous because I considered it self-evident that peace was preferable to war. Then one day I realized that I really did *not* know if it was possible to live in peace. Was I not at war with those who were making war? If I could not live in peace with those whose viewpoints were different from mine, how could I advocate living in peace with persons who actually opposed our democratic way of life?

That was the day I realized that any change I wanted to bring about in the world needed to begin with me. I needed to learn how to live in peace with *my* enemies before I could speak about peace with any authority. I needed to be able to demonstrate how peace works before I could advocate that our nation put down its armaments and live in peace with other nations around the world.

I began that day to focus on building within myself the skills and qualities that a person of peace needs to manifest. This is the awareness that anyone choosing Action as a spiritual Pathway needs to develop.

Look again at the effect you want to see in the world as a result of your action. Then identify the skills you will need to develop and the qualities you will need to manifest to contribute to such an end. These skills and qualities will give you the additional information you need to be able to focus on your purpose in life, and on the objectives you wish to pursue.

For example, if you want to build a world in which cooperation is the norm, rather than competition, you will need to develop your listening skills so that you can hear what people need and want. Communication skills will be essential to helping people develop mutual understanding. You may need organizational skills to bring people together and to help get cooperative projects underway. You will certainly need such qualities as patience, good will, sensitivity, caring, endurance, courage, and objectivity.

## Step Four

Identify your life purpose. This is different from setting a goal. A goal is something specific you set out to do, such as to make health services available to all families living in poverty in your county. A purpose is what motivates you. It is your reason for taking action. It is the over-arching theme that gives meaning to your life. It is a statement of what your life is about and why you are on this planet. A purpose is a comprehensive statement of your conscious direction and intention.

For example, your life purpose might be, as Albert Schweitzer's was, to serve my fellow human beings. Or it might be, to live in peace, or to practice nonviolence, or to embody compassion for all sentient beings. Or you might want to bring harmony wherever you go. Or, to be the change you want to see happen in the world. Or, to heal the planet.

The statement of your life purpose should be large enough to give meaning to everything you do in the course of your life. You are seeking to put into words your deepest longing, your highest value, your true ideal, and to formulate it as an active verb. You want to *do and be* what you want others to have in their lives.

## Step Five

Having identified your life purpose, see if there are additional qualities and skills you will need to fulfill this purpose. Utilizing this list and the one you made under step three above, begin to identify your life objectives. For example, if your life purpose is "to bring harmony wherever I go," some life objectives might be: to develop conflict resolution skills, to learn to listen with an open Heart, to develop patience and humility, to hone my public speaking skills, and to awaken enthusiasm and inspiration at the beginning of each day.

You will notice that your life purpose and your life objectives are all actions that you can take that do not depend on other people. That is, you can get started on them whether anyone joins you or not. This is one of the keys for walking the Path of Action. *You must be able to move forward with your purpose and objectives regardless of the circumstances in which you find yourself.* Even if people oppose you rather than supporting you, you must be able to embody your life purpose. To the extent you are dependent on the support or cooperation of others to embody your purpose, to that extent you are disempowered.


### Step Six

Examine your life. What activities absorb most of your time and attention these days? What motivates you to be involved in these activities? For example, if the majority of your time is spent at work, ask yourself, "Why do I do this work? What drew me to it? What do I hope to accomplish through it?" Your responses to these questions are crucial. *Any* work can serve as your vehicle as you walk the Pathway of Action *if you are using it to express your highest ideals.*

If most of your time right now is spent raising and caring for your children and your life purpose is to bring harmony wherever you go, ask yourself, "Do I live in harmony with my children?" If the answer is no, or only sometimes, then ask yourself what skills or qualities you need to develop to be able to fulfill your life purpose through this work.

If you are employed by a computer software firm and your life purpose is to live in peace, then ask yourself if you are at peace with yourself on the job. Do you resolve conflicts and disagreements with your fellow workers so that peace reigns? Do you radiate peace when you return to your partner and family in the evenings?

The key thing here is to realize that *you are already engaged in your life work*, whatever activities fill the hours of each day. Are you living your life purpose as you engage in your activities? If not, then it is time to realign yourself so that your deepest longings and highest ideals become the focus of your consciousness as you engage in every activity.

If you feel ready to choose the Path of Action as your spiritual discipline, begin to look within. The change you bring to the world will be a reflection of your character. Therefore, you must always ask yourself *why* you are motivated to take action as well as *how* you can bring about the change you seek. Your life should reflect the values you hold.

If you long to be a person of integrity and worth and to realize your hopes for the world around you, then you may indeed have found your Pathway.


## MAKING A COMMITMENT

If you feel confident that you belong on the Pathway of Action, you will want to make a commitment within yourself to do all that you can do to make steady progress on this Path. This commitment is a compact you make with yourself to hold to your highest ideals and to devote yourself to the expression of them in all you do. Though others may join you in work, you are the only one who can monitor your inner life. Even as you collaborate with others in action, you walk your spiritual Path alone. You alone are responsible for your choices, your commitment, your progress, your failures, and your ultimate success.

The Path of Action demands your highest moral integrity. If you have a deep desire to manifest your highest and best in all you do, then you are ready to go deeper in the practices you began as your first steps.

## Why Will You Work?

One who walks the Path of Action knows that through work he can transform the world around him. However, he is also aware that the transformation must begin with self. Using his work as a hammer, he places himself on the anvil of life and begins to mold himself into a perfect expression of his highest ideals.

Mohandas K. Gandhi (1869 - 1948) was a powerful exemplar of this Pathway. He believed that there is no other God than Truth, and he devoted himself to finding the Truth through experiments carried out in his life and work. He came to believe that the only means for the realization of Truth is *ahimsa*, which means the practice of nonviolence.

Gandhi's life purpose was to realize Truth. His principle life objective became to observe *ahimsa* (nonviolence). To observe *ahimsa* he adopted the accompanying objective "to purify myself." Life became his anvil, his life experiments were his hammer, and his deepest desire was to transform himself into a living example of *ahimsa* in mind, word and deed. The causes he took on, such as to gain freedom for his country from British rule or to free the Untouchables from their status as outcasts, constituted the work in which he expressed his purpose and objectives.

Anyone who walks the Pathway of Action is confident that the only way to bring forth the power and knowledge that lie within is through action. As human beings work they bring their inner life force into outer expression, and the real Self within begins to awaken and to recognize its full potential. Only then can that potential be realized.

Therefore, to walk this Pathway is like joining a spiritual health club where you work out in order to strengthen the Divine qualities in your being. Life work affords the opportunity for this workout, this exercise, and thus is a great blessing to you as you walk the Path of Action.

Your ultimate goal as you walk this Pathway is to gain freedom from all bondage, to good as well as to evil. When you are bound up in your ideals, you become rigid within them. You lose your ability to see new possibilities and to adapt to your circumstances. Moreover, you tend to become judgmental of others who do not see things the way you do or hold the same ideals as you do.

When we identify what we consider to be good for ourselves and for the world around us, we can easily become defensive of our ideal. New information and new experiences invite revision of visions of the good. Sitting loose to our own perceptions of what is good and bad may be essential to discovering a larger good.

Until you are free from all that holds you bound to old concepts, beliefs, and patterns, you cannot fully be the change you want to be. You may have developed your old patterns and beliefs before you formulated a clear purpose. To serve your highest ideal you must be free from them.

In his *Autobiography*, Gandhi advocated rising above the opposing currents of love and hatred, attachment and repulsion (504). Gandhi tells of his ceaseless striving for self-purification so that he could live *ahimsa* in mind, word and deed.

When you have identified your highest ideal and formulated your life purpose and supportive objectives, you will want to free yourself from every concept, belief, character pattern, and personality trait that does not support them. The most effective way to free yourself is to focus on bringing into being those qualities, attitudes and beliefs that you have identified as essential if you are to live a life of integrity according to your highest ideal. When our attention is on what we *do* want, what we *don't* want falls away naturally from inattention and lack of expression.

One of the primary reasons you will engage in your life work, then, is to bring forth your own potential to live a life that exemplifies your highest ideal. In other words, you will work in order to become the fullest possible expression of the change you want to see happen in the world. In doing so, you will become an expression of the Divine within you.

It is perhaps helpful to notice that if you walk the Pathway of Action, you engage in your life work and serve the good of humanity in order to free yourself from all that prevents you from knowing your real Self. To state it positively, you work and serve in order to realize your full potential as a microcosm of the Whole, thus becoming a living example of what is possible for all humans.

In contrast, one who walks the Path of *Devotion* serves humanity as an outpouring of Love for God. The focus is not on bringing forth human potential so much as it is on expressing God's unconditional Love for humanity. Thus one on the Pathway of Devotion does not seek to change anything in the world, and is not focused on realizing her own potential. Instead, she seeks to get out of the way so that God's Love might pour through her toward every human with whom she interacts. The work done by devotees on the two Pathways might look similar from the outside, but the motivating forces from within are very different.

## How Will You Work?

Naturally, you will undergo a long process as you walk this Pathway. You will set new intentions, seek to live them out, and then find that you need to do more work on your personality so that you can live out your purposes more fully. What I offer here are general guidelines for that transformational process. You will spiral through these phases according to your own pattern of growth.

## Do What Is Yours to Do

The most important attitude you can cultivate as you walk the Path of Action is to recognize that the power does not lie in the work you do, but in the purpose you bring to that work. As you work with clear intention, bringing your whole self into alignment with your highest ideal, the power of your own character will imprint all with whom you come into contact. Once a reporter asked Mahatma Gandhi for a message to take back to his people. Gandhi replied, "My life is my message." (Black 140) This attitude expresses the commitment adopted by one walking the Path of Action.

For this reason, you will consider whatever work you do to be your opportunity to practice living your own highest ideal. You will start with the life you are already living, entering into every activity, every responsibility, and every task with your life purpose and life objectives in your consciousness, seeking to embody your ideal. You will not wait for the right time or the right opportunity. You will seize *every* opportunity in every here/now moment.

You will trust your own inclination and nature, knowing that the real Self within you arises as tendencies, predispositions and talents even before you bring your highest ideal and life purpose into consciousness. Therefore, if you have been drawn to a particular work because you do it well, trust that that work will serve you in your spiritual development.

You will want to begin a daily practice of preparing for each day by reminding yourself of your life purpose and your life objectives and deciding which specific objective you will focus on for that day. This is important because you want to stay focused on the area of growth that is most challenging to you in each period of your life. These cutting edges will remain in your consciousness for weeks at a time, but when something else surfaces that needs development, you will need to shift your focus to a new objective.

For example, if your life purpose is to embody compassion for all sentient beings, you might be aware that you lack the ability to feel deeply, let alone to feel compassion for all sentient beings. Thus you might adopt as an objective, to breathe into my abdomen and feel. You might practice that objective in the midst of everything you do for many months until you become aware of more feelings and of feeling more deeply.

At that point you might hone the objective, restating it as "to identify my feelings." To identify your feelings you will need to continue to breathe into your abdomen and feel. But in addition, you will need to take time to give a name to the feelings. In this process, which may take many more months, you will discover that there are feelings that support your purpose (such as tenderness, caring, empathy, sadness, happiness, respect, joy, pain) and that there are other feelings that work against your purpose (such as hatred, disdain, pity, anger, impatience, irritation, condescension, frustration, revulsion).

Making this discovery may take you to a next objective, to see beauty in all beings. To practice this objective, you may have to build a new skill, namely, the ability to see through eyes of unconditional love. And as you practice that new skill, you will find that your feelings change. And so the process will continue for you.

At the end of each day, you will want to review

your activities to see how you did at fulfilling your objective. Remember, this review does not focus on the *external* effect of your actions but rather on your *inner alignment* with your intention. Only as you assess yourself will you know what you need to focus on the next day to keep progressing in your efforts to embody your highest ideal.

## Develop the Power of Non-Resistance

In order to find your greatest source of power within, you will want to live your life fully, plunging into the world to suffer and enjoy all that is. As you have a large variety of life experiences and allow yourself to feel deeply the impact of those experiences, you will come to know yourself well in all your patterns and preferences.

It is also important to fulfill your desires so that you do not have hidden or unrecognized needs and wants. Some desires will fall away as you focus on building new qualities and living with a chosen purpose. But others will linger. It is best, then, to fill them as best you can so that they do not weaken your resolve in key circumstances. Desires that can only be met by having a lot of money, for example, can make you susceptible to bribes and compromise. It is better to take time to make money and fill the desires than to undertake a high-minded cause and then find that you can't resist temptations that come your way. Only when you know your patterns and preferences well and fulfill your desires will you be able to stand fast when others try to influence you toward some compromise of your principles or to deter you from your highest ideal and your life purpose.

You are working to become a manifestation of what you consider to be the highest good for yourself and for the world. In order to manifest this good, you need the power to resist all that seems to be its opposite. If you want to serve humanity, you do not want to demand that others serve or obey you. Nor do you want to exhibit selfishness or greed. If you want to live in peace, you do not want to fly into fits of anger or to hold resentments against others. If you want to practice nonviolence, you do not want to lash out at others with words or fists, or to support public policy that oppresses and brings suffering to groups of people. If you want to embody compassion, you do not want to feel hatred, disdain, or pity, or to pass judgment on people who are different from you. If you want to heal the planet, you do not want to poison your property with insecticides or to be wasteful in your consumption of natural resources.

In other words, you want to develop the ability to resist the very life expressions that are the antithesis of your chosen ideal. It is for that reason that you need to know yourself well, fulfill your desires, satisfy your urges, and transform the qualities in your personality. When you have developed the confidence that you will not be pulled off the course of your own purpose by the influence of the opposite of your ideal, you will be able to consider the higher ideal, namely the renunciation of resistance.

Mohandas Gandhi was called "Mahatma," which means "great soul," because of his ability to manifest his highest ideal of *ahimsa* (nonviolence). He learned not to resist violence by discovering through experience that resisting violence only strengthened it. So you will discover that as you resist those actions, attitudes, values and qualities that are the opposite of your ideal, you lend your power to them. They only grow stronger through your opposition.

You will then be in a position, not because you are weak or lazy, but because you will have discovered the futility of resistance, to devote all of your energy to bringing into being what you *want* to see happen, rather than wasting your strength by resisting what you do not want. As you put your energy into the full-hearted living of your highest ideal, you will find that your compassion for others will increase, because you will understand their struggles, their defeats and their victories through your own experience.

### Learn Detachment

One of the paradoxes you will discover is that every action has both good and bad results. I remember in the early days of the movement to save the environment there were groups that banded together to save the redwood trees and to save the dolphins. These appeared to be efforts that could only have good results, since it seemed nothing good would come of denuding the redwood forests or causing the dolphins to become extinct. Yet as the struggle began, it became clear that in both cases thousands of people would lose their livelihood.

In many cases, loggers and tuna fishermen (who inadvertently caught dolphins in their nets and were the primary targets of the movement to save the dolphins) belonged to families that had earned their livelihood in these occupations for generations. Not only was their employment threatened, but an entire way of life. They certainly did not experience this environmental effort as good.

Gandhi had longed to free his people from the

rule of the British Empire. Almost single-handedly, he achieved this goal. But once India was free, a civil war broke out between the Hindus and the Muslims. The Muslims wanted to have their own country and to be free to rule in their own fashion. Thousands of lives were lost in the bloody warfare, and this nearly broke Gandhi's heart. He had longed for his countrymen to be free, but the violence that resulted was the antithesis of his highest ideal.

It is always true that the good brought about by an action is balanced by some evil. For that reason, if you are devoted to walk the Pathway of Action you must remain focused on your motivations and your purpose rather than on the outcome of that action. As Gandhi said:

> By detachment I mean that you must not worry whether the desired result follows from your action or not, so long as your motive is pure, your means correct. Really, it means that things will come right in the end if you take care of the means and leave the rest to Him. (Black 105)

It is easiest to detach from the results of your action if you believe in a personal God and can offer all acts to Him, as those do who walk the Path of Devotion. When you worship God with all you do, then the very act of doing is fulfilling to you. However, even if you do not believe in a personal or transcendent being, you can learn detachment by focusing on the Love that you know in yourself. Do everything as an expression of that Love.

You will discover that the power of Love is the greatest power there is. It has the power to transform, and that transformation will begin with you. As you act through Love, you will be changed. Gandhi said that everything you do in Love will bring you happiness, peace, and a feeling of grace. If what you do does not bring you bliss, then you know you have not acted in Love.

Gandhi used to put the matter bluntly:

> "When another person's welfare means more to you than your own, when even his life means more to you than your own, only then can you say you love. Anything else is just business, give and take. To extend this love even to those who hate you is the farthest limit of *ahimsa* [nonviolence]. It pushes at the boundaries of consciousness itself."
>
> Gandhi was a pioneer in these new realms of consciousness. Everything he did was an experiment in expanding man's capacity to love, and as his capacity grew, the demands on his love grew more and more severe, as if to test what limits a human being can bear. (Black 88)

## Learn the Art of Selflessness

As you express your highest ideal, the change you want to see happen in the world, you will reach out again and again to help others. However, you must do so without expecting to get something for yourself. If you expect any reward, even an expression of gratitude from the ones you have helped, you will set yourself up for disappointment. There will be times when others will praise you for your works, but the praise will be balanced by criticism from your opponents.

There will also be times when you will be paid for your efforts, either monetarily or in special considerations or privileges. However, you must be prepared to carry on even if those rewards are not forthcoming. There will also be times when those who receive benefits from your efforts will thank you. But many others will resent you for helping them or criticize you for not doing more. You must be prepared to stay centered in the Love and compassion that motivate you.

Eventually you will come to recognize that there is no way, ultimately, that you can help any other. If any change is to come about for others, they must become that change from within. As you work, you may provide opportunities for them to step forward and change their own lives. If they do, then change will come about for them. This is part of the genius of the Habitat for Humanity project. Those who will have the privilege of living in and eventually owning one of the homes to be built must participate in the building. By putting forth effort alongside the volunteers that are happy to help them, they actively cooperate in bringing about the change they want to see.

The shortcomings of the Welfare system illustrate the reverse of this principle. Seeking to help those in need, the state has provided financial support. However, until very recently, no effort was made to involve the recipient in the process. Consequently, instead of helping people to better their lives, it most often made them dependent and unable to get off welfare. No one changes unless the change comes from within self.

You will also learn that there is no way to actually improve the world through your actions. That is, there will always be a balance of good and evil, of war and peace, of violence and nonviolence, of creativity and destruction. By your efforts you contribute to maintaining the side of the balance that you want to support. And you will illustrate by your own life that your ideal is a viable alternative for those who are willing to bring it forth from within.

Therefore, you must focus on giving the highest kind of help you can, namely spiritual knowledge. If you teach others the principles on which you are living your life and help them to understand how and why those principles work, you give them knowledge that can truly free them. They, then, must apply that knowledge in their own lives. You cannot do it for them.

One of the most powerful examples of teaching spiritual knowledge came during the Civil Rights Movement of the 1960's. Martin Luther King, Jr. led the movement, not only by setting an example, but also by teaching people the principles of nonviolent resistance. He brought together the teachings of Jesus with the writings and example of Gandhi and helped his people see that they could bring about social change through the power of Love. He said, "Jesus showed us the way. Gandhi showed us it could work." Then he himself set forth a strategy to overcome the evil of segregation with the power of nonviolent resistance and noncooperation. As a result, the entire nation was forced to examine its conscience and inspired to take strides toward creating equal opportunities for all its citizens.

You also give genuine help when you feed the intellect with information that expands understanding and opens the door to new possibilities. Many people are trapped in their patterns and life circumstances because they do not have enough information to realize that they could set change in motion. While Nelson Mandela was in prison for 27 years, he used the time to teach the guards and other prisoners. He taught them how to read. He taught them their own history. He gave them information that helped them to understand how South Africa had come to adopt the practice of Apartheid (separation of the races).

This intellectual training formed the foundation for the change Mandela was able to set in motion when he was finally released from prison. He convinced an entire nation that the only way to move forward, after repealing Apartheid, was to go through a nonviolent process of Truth and Reconciliation. Individuals were invited to come before a panel of authorities to tell their stories of abuse, discrimination, brutality and murder. Those who were accused of perpetrating these crimes were required to be present to hear the stories told. Others were allowed to present further facts as they knew them. Then the accused were invited to come forward so that each could publicly apologize to the aggrieved parties. The aggrieved then publicly forgave them so that both could go forward in their lives.

For the first time in modern history a society resolved long-standing resentments and wounds without retaliation, vengeance or violence. It is almost a miracle, and it could only have happened through the example and leadership of one like Nelson Mandela. Mandela had so much Love in his heart, even for his enemies of many years, that he had no desire for recrimination. Instead, he wanted to devote his energies to setting right what had been wrong. This is the conduct of one who walks the Pathway of Action toward Union with the Divine.

Providing physical help is the most transitory of any kind of help. It meets immediate and urgent needs, but does not address the circumstances that gave rise to those needs, nor does it provide those who are suffering the tools to change what needs to be changed.

This illustrates one of the principle differences between the Paths of Action and of Devotion. Mother Teresa, her feet firmly set on the Path of Devotion, wanted only to express her Love of God by loving the poorest of the poor. She gave them food, cared for them as they were dying, and comforted them in their distress. However, she did not address in any way the social structures and forces that perpetuated their poverty.

On the other hand, Martin Luther King, Jr., walking the Path of Action, expressed his Love for the poor by organizing the War on Poverty. He sought to change social policy in order to provide avenues for the poor to lift themselves up into more fulfilling lives.

Both individuals made enormous contributions to the poor and downtrodden, but in accordance with their chosen Paths, they expressed their Love in quite different ways. As you listen to your own heart, you will come to know what you want to make of your life, and you will find ways to be that change.

## Remember to Give Thanks

Jesus said it is more blessed to give than to receive. This aphorism points to the happiness that comes from being able to give of oneself, one's love, wisdom, knowledge, talents, ideas, and physical efforts. As you walk the Path of Action, you will feel especially grateful for the opportunity to purify and perfect your character through your work.

You will engage in constant efforts to do good primarily because it is a blessing to yourself, in your own spiritual growth, to be able to embody your highest ideal. You will want to remember, therefore, to express your gratitude to the ones you help. Their willingness to receive your efforts enables you to grow into your highest and best self.

The principle effect of the work you do for others is to purify yourself. As you merge with your highest ideal, embodying it at every opportunity, you will experience Union with your real Self and with humanity as a whole. Eventually, giving of yourself in selfless Love will be all you desire.

Gandhi once said:

> Have I that nonviolence of the brave in me? My death alone will show that. If someone killed me and I died with prayer for the assassin on my lips, and God's remembrance and consciousness of His living presence in the sanctuary of my heart, then alone would I be said to have had the nonviolence of the brave. (Black 101)

On the day Gandhi died, he was conducting his customary prayer meeting. The following description of such an evening, from the book *Gandhi the Man*, conveys the transformation that had occurred in Gandhi, enabling him to pass the test he had described and thus to die manifesting the nonviolence of the brave in fulfillment of one of his major objectives.

> His voice was gentle and sweet. It seemed soft but it carried far . . . He wore his body as casually as a cloak, and though it was a frail covering, less than a hundred pounds, the impression he gave was of immense stamina and strength, the measureless force of the spirit. In the gathering dusk the centuries seemed to roll away to reveal

a glimpse of the Compassionate Buddha, giving the secret of nonviolence to a strife-torn world more than twenty-five hundred years before . . .

Mahadev Desai came and sat down near Gandhi and began to read the second chapter of the [Bhagavad] Gita, which describes the perfect man. All his life Gandhi had worked to translate these ideals into his daily life. As the sonorous verses came forth you could see him completely absorbed, his mind growing calm and still and his mighty spirit being released. His concentration was so complete that it was no longer the second chapter you were listening to, it was the second chapter you were seeing, witnessing for yourself the transformation it describes:

> He is forever free who has broken
> Out of the ego-cage of *I* and *mine*
> To be united with the lord of Love.
> This is the supreme state. Attain thou this
> And pass from death to immortality. (Black 139)

On that last evening, a dense crowd had gathered to hear Gandhi speak at the prayer meeting.

As he walked to the platform through the crowd Gandhi held his palms together in front of him in greeting. And as he did so, a young man blinded by hatred placed himself in Gandhi's path, greeting him with the same gesture of his hands, and fired a gun point-blank into Gandhi's heart. Such is the greatness of this little man's love that as his body fell, nothing but the mantra which was deep within him came to his lips, *Rama, Rama, Rama.* It meant *I forgive you, I love you, I bless you.* (Black 140)

Gandhi's life is a perfect example of the way represented by the Pathway of Action. It leads to Union with All through full and compassionate Love and a willingness to give one's life for others.

## THE DANGERS

You will have much support as you walk this Pathway in the West. Hard work wins approval here. People admire men and women of action. There will be many who will want to join you in your efforts. All of this is good. However, there are pitfalls to be avoided if your work is to serve you as a vehicle that will carry you toward Union with All.

Perhaps the largest danger in this society is that you will get lost in the work you are doing and lose sight of why and how you are doing it. Precisely because of your supreme devotion to being the change you want to see happen in the world, it is easy to get caught up in the activity itself and to lose perspective on the reason you are involved in it.

When you choose Action as your Way to spiritual Union, it is not the work that is most important, but rather the transformation that is occurring within you. You must, therefore, always keep your highest ideal in mind and focus on your chosen purposes and objectives. You must, as the Negro Spiritual puts it, "Keep your eye on the prize," and the prize is Union with All, with the Divine. In the end, the work itself falls away and what is left is what you have *become* in the process.

A second danger is that you will become successful at what you do and begin to take pride in your accomplishments. The change is subtle, but when you feel pride, your attention shifts from the ideal and your purpose to yourself. You begin to believe that *you* have wrought changes in the world around you, forgetting that the only thing you have the power to change is yourself. Any other change that occurs is due to choices others have made and to the movements of large currents of energy in the group as a whole.

If you focus on yourself and your own accomplishments, you will lose your ability to Love unconditionally and to pour your energy out in service to others. Rather than merging with others in expression of your oneness, you will set yourself apart as the one who knows, the one who is effective, the one who achieves. Any of these attitudes will cause you to diverge from your journey toward Union with the Divine.

The antidote to this danger is gratitude. Whenever you are successful, breathe into your heart and express gratitude for the privilege of working toward this end. Express your gratitude that you were able to be of some service and that you had the privilege of bringing your influence to bear on this situation or these individuals. When your heart wells up with gratitude you cannot fall into pride because you experience yourself as a small part of a much larger whole.

Another equal danger for the disciple on the Pathway of Action is that you will become discouraged and feel like a failure. This is the same temptation in its opposite polarity. Your focus has shifted to the goal, and the fact that you have not reached it has caused you to lose heart. Again, gratitude for what you are learning in the process and for the opportunity to do your spiritual work in this way will keep you centered on your purpose.

Mahatma Gandhi once said:

> The goal ever recedes from us. The greater the progress, the greater the recognition of our unworthiness. Satisfaction lies in the effort, not in the attainment. Full effort is full victory." (Black 102)

This attitude keeps your attention focused on *how* you are working rather than on whether you have succeeded in your work. The closer you come to attaining your first goal, the more you will see there is to do. Your perspective on each situation changes as you progress; consequently your understanding changes. In this way, you find that there is always more to do.

One other danger is that as you walk this Pathway you will begin to recognize the power you are able to bring forth from within yourself. Others will acknowledge this power in you. They may admire you for it, or they may fear you. Either way, they will set you apart from themselves, feeling weaker because of your strength.

Your challenge is to stay centered in Love, not power. Love is powerful, but it does not disempower others. To the contrary, Love binds people together in a feeling of solidarity and oneness. As you build up the force of Love within, you must recognize that it is *Love* that is powerful, not you or your efforts.

It is essential, then, as a disciple walking the Pathway of Action to keep your attention focused on your highest ideal and to keep measuring yourself against it. Your deepest longing must be to embody that ideal. Sustain your efforts in your work in the world in order to bring forth from yourself the qualities and skills that will enable you to be the change you want to see in the world.

## SUMMARY

To characterize the Path of Action in summary, then, we could say that this is the way of the humanitarian change agent. In our Western society, you will be acknowledged and supported by those around you as you set out on this Path, for ours is a culture that values practical and effective action. However, others will not necessarily understand or support your intention to use your work as a spiritual practice.

As a spiritual discipline, the Path of Action asks that as you work you purify your character so that the motivations that drive you are characterized by unconditional Love.

As you walk this Path you must seek to embody your highest ideal in all situations and under all circumstances. Only you know what that ideal is and only you can assess whether you are living up to it.

Second, you must learn the art of nonresistance. When you have a strong ideal, it is a temptation to throw up resistance to all that seems in opposition to your ideal. But as you walk the Pathway of Action, you learn that resistance only strengthens the opposition, whereas nonresistance frees you to put all your energy into being the change you want to see happen in the world.

Third, you must learn to Love unconditionally and universally so that your every action becomes an expression of Love that frees others to bring forth the fullness of their potential from within. You must learn to Love yourself as unconditionally as you Love others, because only by doing so are you free from the need to be loved by others.

Fourth, you must learn to renounce the fruits of

your action. That is, you must expect nothing to come to you in return, not even gratitude. Knowing that your actions cannot be purely good, you must let go of the need to see the results you intend. Rather you must act only because you love to act in Love.

By working in these ways, you will overcome the heartache and disillusionment of seeking to accomplish something in the world and never being enough or doing enough. You will bring yourself to recognize your oneness with all humans, no matter what their circumstance or character, and you will rejoice in the power you have to transform your own life and through that transformation to bring about change in the world around you.

As you live fully with passion and zest and do your work with a light heart, in both gratitude and joy, you will find yourself enjoying Union with All. You will enjoy the Divine delight of heaven right here and now in this world with all its seeming imperfections.

**Works Cited:**

Black, Jo Anne, Nick Harvey, and Laurel Robertson. *Gandhi the Man.* San Francisco: Glide Publications, 1972.

Gandhi, Mohandas K. *An Autobiography: The Story of My Experiments with Truth.* Boston: Beacon Press, 1957.

# THE PATH OF CONTEMPLATION
## A SEARCH for KNOWLEDGE of the TRUE and REAL

*You shall know the Truth,*
*and the Truth will set you free.*
                    *— John 8:32*

This is a mental Pathway, using the mind to pursue what the mind can never know. It is the most suitable Pathway for those who show a natural inclination to transcend their limited states of awareness through the use of reason and abstract thought. Often such persons pursue conceptual realms that would leave most people's heads swimming. It is as though they use language to escape the limitations of the senses. Then the language itself serves as the tool by which they stop thinking and come to direct knowing.

The Path of Contemplation will serve you if you are predisposed to ponder the imponderable, to reflect deeply on the large questions of life, and to question all answers no matter how profound they might seem. If it is your natural inclination to reason, to think and to contemplate, and you use the intellect as your primary tool as you approach life, this may be your Path.

The Path of Contemplation has not had a prominent place in religious life in the West. Most individuals predisposed to this Pathway have pursued secular careers in science and philosophy, or academic careers in their chosen fields. The few who have remained within Christianity have gone into monasteries where contemplation is respected or, in both Judaism and Christianity, have taken up teaching in theological seminaries where the mind is held in high regard.

If you have been drawn to Talmudic studies within Judaism or to studies of theology within Christianity, or if you have been attracted to Buddhism in one of its many expressions, this Pathway may serve you well on your journey Home. If, on the other hand, you find philosophical discussions boring because they do not seem to open the Heart or take feelings into account, you may find the Path of Devotion more to your liking. If you have little patience for discussion that does not result in endeavors that will benefit humanity in some practical way, you will probably find the Pathway of Action suits you better. Or if you long to know how to apply any knowledge you gain to your own life and self-expression, then you may be more at home with the Path of Self-Mastery.

If you think this is probably *not* your Path, you may want to turn now to another chapter. If you do that, I encourage you to come back later to this chapter so that you can better understand those who are, by nature, disposed to contemplation. Reading this chapter will help you to love and appreciate them for who they are and for the longings that motivate them on their way Home.

# FIRST STEPS ON THE PATH

If you walk the Path of Contemplation toward Union with the Divine, you will be known as a philosopher, a lover of wisdom, one who longs to know through direct perception, through identity with the knowledge, through oneness with what you come to know.

Knowledge about the nature of reality learned from others and based on their experience will not satisfy you. You do not want to know *about* reality; you want to *know* the Real and the True. There is a difference.

This is a rigorous Path that requires mental discipline. You will need a sound and healthy body and a balanced emotional life to be able to integrate the fruits of your mental quest. You will quickly discover whether this kind of discipline thrills you or exhausts you. So if you believe that the Pathway of Contemplation will serve you to find Union with the Absolute, that which is beyond all words and definitions, take your first steps and you will know.

## Step One:

Sharpen your mind as if it were a tool. If you are drawn to this Pathway, you probably learned to discipline your mind as you went through school or pursued your own reading, and you may have learned the rules of logic. If not, take time to do so. You will need to know how to think things through in such a way that you do not deceive yourself with false reasoning. Philosophers through the ages have developed certain rules of logic that will help you to stay on your course. Take a class, read a book, or find someone to mentor you. Learn how to think constructively.

## Step Two:

Learn conscious abstracting. We humans use language for most of our reasoning, and it is important that you understand how language relates to reality. A study of General Semantics, or conscious abstracting, will help you to understand your thought process. Take a course in General Semantics or read some of the books that are readily available.[1]

## Step Three:

Learn how to work with numbers as a symbolic key to the principles underlying the cosmos. The study of algebra and trigonometry is a beginning of such knowledge. If you enjoy math, continue your study of abstract thinking through the use of mathematical formulas. You may also want to investigate the use of numbers as symbols to represent philosophical concepts and perceptions.[2]

## Step Four:

Examine your deepest longings. Do you long to know what is True in the deepest sense? Do you want to perceive what is Real? Do you want to live your life in accordance with what is True? What purpose will your knowledge serve?

As you reflect on these questions, make notes of your findings. Begin to develop your own philosophy of life, if you have not already done so. Write what is true for you and what you long to know. Write your purpose for living and your purpose for knowing. Then keep referring back to what you have written. Revise your purpose whenever it is appropriate in the light of further reflection and study.

### Step Five:
Read the writings of great philosophers like Plato, Kierkegaard, Hegel, Schopenhauer, Nietzsche, Descartes, Bertrand Russell and Immanuel Kant. Use this reading to practice concentration as you focus on their lines of reasoning until you can follow them with little effort. As you discover what questions most engage you, pursue those in steps Six and Seven.

### Step Six:
Contemplate those matters that most concern or interest you. For example, you may want to know, "What is the nature of being human?" or "Why are human beings prone to cruelty and violence?" Take the question into the silence of your inner being. Think deeply about it. Follow lines of reason to their ends. Then continue to contemplate the question, not settling for any answer you can formulate with your mind, yet seeking to understand, to know. Hold the question in the back of your mind as you go through your days, using every experience as further data for your inquiry. When insights come, write them down and then continue to contemplate the question. Stretch to the very limits of your mental capacity, and then continue the search.

Franklin Merrell-Wolff (1887-1985), a mathematician, physicist and philosopher who walked this Pathway, wrote about his state of meditation:

I was . . . thinking thoughts that were so abstract that there were no concepts to represent them. I seemed to comprehend a veritable library of Knowledge, all less concrete than the most abstract mathematics. (5)

Stretch yourself in that direction.

## Step Seven:

Begin with a simple question such as *Who Am I?* Acknowledge that the answer to this question may hold the key to your liberation from not-knowing. One of the great twentieth century *Jnana*-Yogis in India, walking the Pathway of Contemplation, was Sri Nisargadatta Maharaj. In his book *I Am That* he said:

> The seeker is he who is in search of himself.
>
> Give up all questions except one: "Who am I?" After all, the only fact you are sure of is that you are. The "I am" is certain. The "I am this" is not. Struggle to find out what you are in reality.
>
> Use your reason to pursue the question as far as you possibly can with thought.
>
> Discover all that you are not—body, feelings, thoughts, time, space, this or that—nothing, concrete or abstract, which you perceive can be you. The very act of perceiving shows that you are not what you perceive. (vi)

As you reason, sustain your concentration upon the original question *Who Am I?* Do not let the mind go far afield. Keep it focused, its reasoning directly related to the question.

When you have gone as far as you can go with thinking, hold the question in the foreground of your awareness and go into deep meditation on it, now no longer thinking about it, but contemplating it and eventually becoming one with it.

> The clearer you understand that on the level of mind you can be described in negative terms only, the quicker will you come to the end of your search and realize that you are the limitless being. (Nisargadatta, vi)

If you find that these initial steps on the Pathway of Contemplation come naturally to you, if you respond to them with satisfaction and feel the thrill of the pursuit of Truth through reason, and if you have begun to experience the stillness of Home in your meditation, then you may indeed have found your Path. Others are likely to find this Pathway too exacting, even sterile. But for the lover of wisdom, it is as though the body has a hunger and the feeling nature a deep desire or longing for that which only the mind can pursue.

## MAKING A COMMITMENT

If you feel confident that you belong on the Path of Contemplation, make a deep commitment within to pursue Union with the Divine on this Path. An insatiable desire to know will sustain you through dry and arid mental terrain. There are few emotional or physical *pleasures* for the lover of wisdom, though you will feel a deep *satisfaction* as you pursue. You will be focused on lifting the energies of the throat chakra,[3] that is, the thinking and conceptualizing of your objective state of consciousness, into the third eye chakra. It is in the third eye chakra that your seeing, insight, and understanding occur. There, images-appearing-substantive, our ordinary way of seeing the world, will dissolve into direct perception of Reality. In that mode you will see no images. The body and emotions need to remain still and unobtrusive for this kind of inner work to be done.

If you are committed to follow your passion to know what is True and Real, then you are ready to go further on the Path of Contemplation.

## Discriminate between the Real and the Unreal

To walk the Path of Contemplation you must develop three primary disciplines. The first is the discipline of *discriminating between the Real and the unreal.*

Human consciousness is focused on a seemingly objective reality. We see our world as composed of objects that can be detected by seeing, hearing, touching, smelling, or tasting. And we believe ourselves to be objects in this objective world. Our world is out there, separate from us, and we are separate objects within that world. That world, we believe, is real.

The West is preoccupied with this so-called material world. We have not allowed our prevailing objective world view to be shaken by physicists who tell us that this is an *energy world* and that objects are not really solid at all. Whirling molecules comprise these seemingly solid objects. Nor does it seem to disturb us that we place our faith in chemical substances that work miracles of healing in our bodies even though we cannot see them, feel them, touch them, smell them or taste them. We struggle to overcome stress created by emotional and mental energies that are not physical, addressing evidence of the stress as we identify it in our physical bodies. Yet we persist in doubting that anything not perceptible to our five senses is real.

Your first challenge as you walk the Pathway of Contemplation is to break out of this world view. The science of General Semantics will help you to understand how we have fallen into the trap of believing that the images in our psyches (personality fields) are *out there*. The inability of our nervous systems at their present state of development to register the rapidity of the wave-frequencies of the energy world causes us to perceive gestalts that do not exist except in our psyches, where we store them in memory and refer to them.

Not only do we abstract images from the energetic reality, we also name or label the images, and classify them according to qualities and attributes that we define as distinguishing. And as we move into higher and higher orders of abstraction, we return less and less to the Reality from which we began the abstracting process.

For example, we carry an image of "tree" in our psyches. We have a specific name, such as "pine tree." Then we identify the pine tree as a "conifer" because it bears cones, and as an "evergreen" because it stays green all year round. The pine tree is also a "plant," a much broader category that includes more than trees. When we say that the pine tree is a "living thing" we have moved to an even higher order of abstraction. The category "living" includes everything except what is "not living."

Drawing the distinction between the two categories becomes very complex and involves concepts more than direct experience. By the time we start to talk about the "life force" in living things, we are at a level of abstraction that makes it impossible to point to anything we can register with our senses or perceive in energy.

As we engage in this process of abstraction, we create private worlds of illusion. We live *as if* our picture-images of reality were real. This is what has been called *the maya* in Eastern philosophies. It is our waking dream and we are completely absorbed in it. If you want to know more about this phenomenon, read *Life As A Waking Dream*.[4]

Your first discipline will be to learn to discriminate between the Real and the unreal. Understanding how the mind works and learning the rules of logic will help you to sort through your illusions. To learn to perceive the Real, you will have to learn to think without passing judgment. You will have to let go of thinking and merge with Reality to learn to meditate

One of the great exemplars of the Path of Contemplation was J. Krishnamurti (1895-1986). Born in India, Krishnamurti was adopted by Annie Besant and raised to be the new World Teacher, a reincarnation of the Buddha for the new millennium. He would not accept the title because he felt it encumbered him with too many expectations and images that were part of the traditions of the past. Nevertheless, for more than sixty years he traveled all over the world giving public talks and private interviews to millions of people. He taught that people must not look to him as the one who could bring about change. He said change would only come about in society, and peace would only reign in the world, when a complete change came about in the hearts and minds of individuals.

Rather than found a new religion, Krishnamurti embodied a spiritual Pathway. He made it clear that he could not do the work of spiritual unfoldment for anyone else; all individuals must make their own way toward spiritual Union.

Krishnamurti's message was always conveyed in a style typical of one walking the Path of Contemplation. He engaged the mind and then stretched it to its limits. During a conversation in San Diego, California on February 28, 1974, made available on the Krishnamurti Information Network's website,[5] Dr. Allan W. Anderson asked, "What is meditation?" Krishnamurti responded, "We can proceed and investigate together, and therefore share together this question of what is meditation . . . if we start with saying that we really do not know what meditation is."

In this way, Krishnamurti laid the groundwork for the kind of inquiry that serves as contemplation. To contemplate a question such as "what is meditation?" you begin by acknowledging that you do not know what it is. None of the information you have about meditation can serve you in this inquiry. No one else's experience or description or prescription will help you. If you are to contemplate this question, you must begin from ground zero: I do not know what meditation is. Krishnamurti said that the attitude of "I don't know" brings an acknowledgment of "freedom from the established known, the established traditions, the established methods, the established schools and practices." Without that freedom, any inquiry would be mere pretense.

On another occasion, Krishnamurti said:

To dig deeply you must have the right instrument,

not merely the desire to dig . . . To cultivate the right instrument of perception, thought must cease to condemn,
to deny, to compare and judge or seek comfort or security. (Lutyens 61)

So, the thought process must be freed of all past
influences and of judgments and preferences if you are
to deeply contemplate any subject.

Once you have acknowledged that you do not
know, then you may begin to explore by probing with
one question after another. Here are excerpts from
Krishnamurti's exploration with Dr. Anderson of what
meditation is:

> I start with something I don't know. For me that has
> great beauty. Then I am free to move. I'm free to flow, or
> swim, within the enquiry. So, I don't know. Now then,
> from that we can start.
>
> First of all, is meditation divorced from daily living?
> The daily conduct, the daily desires of fulfillment, ambi-
> tion, greed, envy, the daily competitive, imitative, con-
> forming spirit, the daily appetites, sensual, sexual, other
> forms, intellectual and so on. Is meditation divorced from
> all that? Or does meditation flow through all that, cover
> all that, include all that? If it is divorced from life then
> meditation has no meaning. It's just an escape from life,
> escape from all our travails and miseries, sorrows, confu-
> sions. And therefore it's not worth even touching.
>
> If it is not, and it is not for me, then what is medita-
> tion? Is it an achievement, an attainment of a goal? Or is
> it a perfume, a beauty that pervades all my activities? . . .
>
> And also there is the question of sleep. I go to sleep,
> eight, nine, ten hours. What is sleep? I start not knowing.
>
> . . . I'm enquiring in relation to meditation, which is
> the real spirit of religion. That is, gathering all the energy
> to move from one dimension to a totally different dimen-
> sion. Which doesn't mean divorce from this dimension . .

So, what is sleep? And what is waking? Am I awake? Or, am I only awake when there is a crisis, when there is a shock, when there is a challenge, when there is an incident, death, discard, or failure? Or am I awake all the time, in waking during the daytime? So what is it to be awake?

So, in my enquiry I am asking, am I awake? What does it mean to be awake? I am not awake if I have any burden. There is no sense of being awake when there is any kind of fear. If I live with an illusion, if my actions are neurotic, there is no state of being awake. So I'm enquiring and I can only enquire by becoming very sensitive to what is happening in me, outside me. So is the mind aware during the day completely to what is happening inside, outside of me?

Am I awake? Or is the past so alive that it is dictating my life in the present? Therefore I am asleep . . . Because I'm talking from the background of my past, of my experience, of my failures, my hurts, my depressions; therefore the past is dominating and putting me to sleep now. When the past covers the present, then I am asleep . . .

Then what is sleep? I have understood now what it means to be awake. That means I am watching. I am aware. I am aware without any choice, choiceless awareness, watching, looking, observing, hearing, what is going on and what is going outside, what people tell me, whether they flatter me, or they insult me. I am watching. So I am very aware.

Now, what is sleep? (Website)

And so Krishnamurti's inquiry continues until the mind has explored all the ramifications of the question, "What is meditation?" All of this is contemplation. In contemplation you hold one thought or question and explore it until you have exhausted all thought. The mind is stretched to its limits. Then it falls into silence, and in the silence meditation begins.

On another occasion Krishnamurti wrote:

> Meditation is one of the greatest arts in life — perhaps *the* greatest, and one cannot possibly learn it from anybody. That is the beauty of it. It has no technique and therefore no authority. When you learn about yourself, watch yourself, watch the way you walk, how you eat, what you say, the gossip, the hate, the jealousy — if you are aware of all that in yourself, without any choice, that is part of meditation. So meditation can take place when you are sitting in a bus or walking in the woods full of light and shadows, or listening to the singing of birds or looking at the face of your wife or child. (Lutyens 59)[6]

Meditation is choiceless awareness, according to Krishnamurti. But it is more than that. It is acute attentiveness to the actual moment of perception without any separation from what is being perceived. When the perceiver and the perceived are one, then it is possible to know what is Real.

These words by Krishnamurti, written in 1980, elucidate this understanding of meditation even further:

> When man becomes aware of the movement of his own consciousness he will see the division between the thinker and the thought, the observer and the observed, the experiencer and the experience. He will discover that this division is an illusion. Then only is there pure observation, which is insight without any shadow of the past. This timeless insight brings about a deep radical change in the mind. (Lutyens 205)

The radical change in the mind is a state of

Union, of unity, of oneness. And in that unitary consciousness, all duality, all separation, is recognized as
unreal. On another occasion Krishnamurti said:

> When I understand myself, then there is quietness,
> then there is stillness of the mind. In that stillness, reality
> can come to me. That stillness is not stagnation, is not a
> denial of action. On the contrary it is the highest form of
> action. In that stillness there is creation — not the mere
> expression of a particular creative activity, but the feeling
> of creation itself. (Lutyens 77)

With such words Krishnamurti attempts to express what he has come to know through his meditative states. But his words cannot give you that knowing. You must learn to discriminate for yourself between the Real and the unreal. This is the first major
discipline on the Path of Contemplation.

## Exercise Self-Control, Directing the Mind Toward Reality

The second discipline you must adopt as you
walk the Path of Contemplation is *self-control*. Once
you have caught a glimpse of Reality, your challenge
will be to continue to direct your mind toward Reality,
rather than allowing it to slip back into identification
with the unreal. To do this requires enormous self-
control because the habits, not only of *your* lifetime,
but also of the entire history of humanity, will weigh
on you, pulling you back toward the familiar realm of
illusion.

Gautama Buddha, the supreme example of this

Pathway, advocated three practices to control the mind: Right Effort, Right Mindfulness (or Awareness), and Right Meditation. By **Right Effort** he meant to exercise self-discipline with regard to the life of the senses, or what we have called objective life. If you allow yourself to fall back into the habit of believing that the images abstracted from your sensory impressions are real, then you will fall back into duality, perceiving yourself as separate from the world out there. Therefore, you will need to discipline yourself to remain aware of how the mind works in objective awareness so that you abstract consciously and do not forget that your images and thoughts are *not* the reality from which they were abstracted.

Moreover, you will need to discipline yourself not to arouse passion in relation to those images, whether they are visual, mental or emotional. When you begin to feel deeply about the images, you fall into waking dreams. You become absorbed in the content of those waking dreams. You are like Don Quixote, swinging your sword at the windmills of your mind. Your passion must be only for knowledge of the Real and the True.

**Right Mindfulness** (or Awareness) engages reason to reflect on the traps that are inherent in clinging to the illusion of a world of objects. As you direct your mind to the Real, you must be on alert for ways you delude yourself, even in the subtlest ways. For example, to desire liberation from suffering, or inspiration, or even knowledge of the Real can create a separation that will prevent you from attaining what you desire. When you desire something, you are really pursuing an image in your psyche, some idea you have of what liberation or Truth is.

The active way of avoiding such traps is to constantly move from what you *think* you know to the recognition that you *do not know*. To recognize that every answer you have found cannot be the Truth. To question every answer. To constantly probe behind what you already see. In this way, you keep directing the mind to move past all images, all concepts, and all thoughts, into the unknown where you can directly perceive the Real.

The passive way to avoid the traps inherent in the objective reality is to let go of every desire, every aspiration, every goal, and simply be present to what is. This is the choiceless awareness that Krishnamurti talked about, awareness from moment to moment of all that is taking place inside and outside oneself without any effort to direct or change it. Krishnamurti taught that this pure observation, or direct perception, would result in a transformation of the mind without any effort toward that end.

**Right Meditation**, according to Gautama, keeps the mind concentrated in spiritual contemplation in order to free it from all thought and, transcending thought, to attain the state of Union. Spiritual contemplation is the manner of pursuing knowledge that we started with above, in which you seek to discriminate between the Real and the unreal, and in that way, to know Truth.

## Detach the True Self from the Non-Self

According to Gautama Buddha, **Right Understanding** is the proper grasp of the problem of existence. Central to that understanding is the awareness that we cling to a false self, a self that is seen as separate from others and the world around us. To live in Reality, you must *let go of your identification with the false self.* Gautama taught that the aspiration to renounce the false self is **Right Purpose** and would enable one to step on the Path to freedom from all suffering.

The false self is what most people would call the personality. It includes the body when it is related to as objective, or physical. The personality is a false self because it is seen as separate, and because it is actually only a bundle of images and impressions held in the psyche (in feelings and thoughts). To identify ourselves, or anyone else, we describe the body, or rather our image of the body, and the patterns of behavior that characterize the person. We might say, "Dave is a tall, skinny guy with spiky red hair and a temper to match." We can do this only by referring to our past experiences and impressions. None of them address the Real Self, which is always and only knowable in the present moment.

As you walk this Path, you must learn to identify with the Real Self, which is not an image, not past expressions, not any content held within the psyche. The Real Self is the power with which you are conscious. There is no separation between the Real Self and the One, or the All. Consequently, to identify with the Real Self is to enter unity consciousness.

To discipline yourself to identify with the Real Self, Gautama Buddha advocated relating to others and the world around you as if you were One with them. This attitude is expressed through Right Speech, Right Conduct, and Right Livelihood.

**Right speech** is the principle of speaking Truth. As you walk this Pathway you are devoted to knowing the Truth. To the degree that you come to know that in Reality you are not separate from others, you can begin to speak the Truth of that awareness. When you address others while experiencing Union, your words will engender the trust that comes from knowing that you do not stand in opposition to the other, but rather in oneness with them. You will develop the skills of a peacemaker, a bridge-builder, one who is able to bring people together who have been divided.

Tenzin Gyatso, the fourteenth Dalai Lama of Tibet, is a superb example of Right Speech. He has occasion to speak Truth all around the world, and wherever he goes, people recognize that he does not set himself apart from them. They sense that he understands the human condition and that he wants what is best for all humans. Even when he talks about the Chinese, who as of this year 2001 continue to rule over Tibet, he speaks without malice and with respect. It is no surprise that the Dalai Lama was awarded a Nobel Peace Prize for his efforts at reconciliation. He never allows his false self (the sense of being a separate individual) to interfere with his communication of the Truth that we are all One.

**Right conduct** is living out the Truth of unity consciousness in action. Buddhists often speak of having compassion for all sentient beings. This attitude of compassion is an organic response to the recognition that all beings are expressions of the One Self. To cause harm to any living creature would be to bring suffering to the Whole. Therefore, empathetic kindness becomes a universal orientation for one walking this Pathway.

This means that to live out the Truth that you are not a separate entity, you give up all desire to have for yourself what you would not also give to all others. It means that you have concern for the needs of others as you would for your own needs. It means that you watch out for the well-being of all living creatures. It means that you would not consider taking the life of another to preserve your own.

**Right livelihood** simply means earning your living from a work that does not harm others. Many jobs today, although not directly harmful to others, contribute to the manufacture of weapons, to the pollution of the environment, or to the exploitation of workers in some other locale. It often takes research to discover whether you are being paid for efforts that eventually harm others. But to be consistent with your purpose of knowing what is True and Real, making such a determination is essential.

The intention to align your external conduct with your stated life purpose provides a moral foundation that enables your deeper spiritual work to be pursued. To observe your words, actions, and daily work to make sure they are consistent with the Truth as you know it at each step along the way will require that you remain detached from your personal, or false, self. Others might experience this impersonality as cold or calculated. However, it need not be.

Krishnamurti once said:

> Love can only be when the sense of the self is absent, and freedom from the self lies through self-knowledge. With self-knowledge there comes understanding; and when the total process of the mind is fully revealed and understood, then you will know what it is to love. Then you will see that love is not a means of fulfillment . . . . Love is a state of being. (Lutyens 78)

During a conversation on another occasion, Krishnamurti said:

> You asked me just now about personal love, and my answer is that I no longer know it. Personal love does not exist for me. Love is for me a constant inner state. People sometimes think that I am superficial and cold. But it is not indifference, it is merely a feeling of love that is constantly within me and that I simply cannot help giving to everyone that I come into touch with. (Lutyens 33)

To detach the True Self from the false self results in falling into a state of Love that is constant, and from that Love emanates kindness and compassion toward all beings. From within that constant Love it becomes impossible to speak words that separate you from others, or to do harm to others through your actions or work. Instead, you become an instrument of peace in the world, building bridges by who you are as well as by what you say and do.

Sri Aurobindo (1872-1950), one of the great philosophers of the twentieth century and an exemplar of the Path of Contemplation, described the state of detaching the True Self from the false self like this:

> Above my head a mighty head was seen,
> A face with the calm of immortality
> And an omnipotent gaze that held the scene
> In the vast circle of its sovereignty.
> His hair was mingled with the sun and breeze;
> The world was in His heart and He was I:
> I housed in me the Everlasting's peace,
> *The strength of One whose substance cannot die.*[7]

## THE DANGERS

Of all the Pathways, this is perhaps the most difficult because it is so solitary. All of your attention is directed inward, into your own mind and consciousness. This means that you have virtually no support from others around you. They may find you aloof, unfeeling, detached, uncaring, indifferent, and even arrogant. Thus, to walk this Pathway you must have a great deal of inner fortitude.

One of the dangers is that you will build up a wall of self-protection against the criticism of others. Not only may they criticize you for being so impersonal that you seem not to care about them, but they may also criticize your quest for Truth as self-absorbed naval-gazing that makes no contribution to the world around you. If you seek to protect yourself from such criticism, you not only isolate yourself from your critics, but you erect a large barrier to your own search for Truth.  Since Reality is unitary according to all the great perceivers, a wall which protects you also separates you from the Reality you most long to know.

Another danger is that you will get lost on the mental level, which is by nature characterized by dualism. The paradox of this Pathway is that you will use thought processes to transcend the mental. That is, you will think your way through to the realm of no thought. However, if you become so sophisticated in your thinking that you create an abstract image of the void, the realm beyond thought, then you will delude yourself into thinking that you have broken free of the mental when you are actually trapped in it.

Perhaps the only sure way to avoid this trap is to find a teacher who has found liberation. Such a one will not be deceived by any imitation of the Real and the True and will be able to awaken you to your own illusion if you fall into it. How can you find such a teacher? Follow your intuition. Read. Ask. Listen inwardly. Be patient.

If you have no teacher, there is another way to test the validity of your own perceptions. Go out into the world and interact with ordinary human beings. As you work with others, establish friendships with them, marry, have children, and in all other ways live an ordinary life, you will very quickly discover whether you are free. If you do not get caught in reactions, if you sustain your feeling of solidarity with these others, if your inner peace and tranquility remains undisturbed, then you will know that you are free.

If, on the other hand, you find yourself annoyed, impatient, angry, or frustrated, or if longing and desire are awakened in you, you can be sure that you are still identified to some degree with the false self. You will find teachers in all who unintentionally challenge your sense of freedom. To the degree they disturb you in any way, to that degree they are serving you in your quest for the ultimate Truth that brings liberation.

A third danger on this Pathway is, in fact, that you will isolate yourself from other human beings. The nature of your quest is solitary and most of your methods will be best employed when you are alone. However, to cut yourself off from relationships completely, or for too long a time, is to live an untruth. Such isolation can serve you as you learn to enter deep meditative states, but if sustained too long, it violates the Truth that you are, in Reality, One with all others.

Therefore, you must challenge yourself to stay in the world and live the Truth you come to know. Sri

Aurobindo, the great Indian sage, brought the message:

> One need not leave the earth to find the Truth, one need not leave the life to find his soul, one need not abandon the world or have only limited beliefs to enter into relation with the Divine. The Divine is everywhere, in everything, and if He is hidden, it is because we do not take the trouble to discover Him.[8]

Finally, there is the danger that you will perceive the Truth but fail to integrate it into your own personal expression. To *know* the Truth is not enough. You must also *be* the Truth. Asoka, the great Buddhist emperor of India (274-232 B.C.), who sent missionaries to many countries to spread the teachings of Gautama, described the qualities of being that result from achieving enlightenment. He said that one who is liberated is characterized by compassion, liberality, truth, purity, gentleness, peace, joyousness, saintliness, and self-control (Prabhavananda 180). These are qualities that manifest in the personality, even though the one who has found liberation is no longer attached to his personal self. St. Paul, the great Christian missionary, listed very similar qualities as "fruits of the spirit." He called them love, joy, peace, patience, kindness, goodness, fidelity, gentleness, and self-control (Gal. 5:6).

If you walk this Path, you must observe yourself in your human interactions in the world. If the qualities listed above, according to Asoka and to St. Paul, are not manifest in your self-expression, then you may have fallen into the trap of believing that knowledge alone is sufficient. It is not. You must be willing to let your whole self be transformed by what you have come to know. As Krishnamurti put it, "The attainment of Truth is an absolute, final experience. I have recreated myself after Truth" (Lutyens 31). He was *being* the Truth he came to know, and so must you.

## SUMMARY

In summary, the Pathway of Contemplation is the way of the philosopher, the mathematician, the theoretical scientist, and the logician. Those who walk this way are the essentially invisible Truth-seekers of our Western culture who do not command a great deal of respect or receive a great deal of support because their quest does not appear to be pragmatic. The theoretical is of little interest in our culture until we have evidence of its practical application to our daily lives.

By nature, this is a solitary Path, but the lack of understanding and support it commands in our culture make it even more so. It is, therefore, only for those whose thirst for knowledge of the True and Real is so powerful that they have no choice but to pursue their inward journey.

Your life purpose as you walk this way is, as for disciples on all Paths, to come to Union with the Ineffable. On this Pathway, God is understood to be a transcendent Reality beyond all grasp of the senses and of human reason, beyond time and space, beyond all divisions and separations, and beyond all existence. The objects of human desires, of the attention of the senses, and of our thought processes are understood to be illusion. They constitute the false and the unreal. You have a secondary purpose on this Pathway, then, which is to know the True and the Real by becoming one with it.

In response to an inner urge to find the ultimate meaning of life, to know the Truth, to know what is Real, you set the intention to learn to discriminate between the Real and the unreal through analysis and reason. This requires that you exercise a great deal of self-control in order to be able to direct the mind towards Reality and to detach the true Self from the non-self.

You will use the mind as your primary tool and develop the skills of concentration, contemplation and meditation. A healthy body and a balanced personal life will facilitate the stilling of the senses, an essential factor in being able to direct the mind toward Reality. And as your mind falls into silence you will find yourself dwelling in a void in which peace and Love prevail. The Reality you perceive in that state will work a transformation in your personal self that will be expressed as the radiant fruits of the spirit.

Knowing the Truth will set you free from all illusion and suffering and give you inward peace and strength. The joy of complete oneness with the Real will be expressed through you as Love and compassion toward all creatures in the universe. In these ways you will *become* the Truth you contemplate. You will be a living expression of all that is Real and True.

---

1. See, for example, *Drive Yourself Sane: Using the Uncommon Sense of General Semantics,* by Bruce I. and Susan Presby Kodish, Extensional Publishing, 2000.

2. See, for example, Sepharial, *The Kabala of Numbers Part 1,* North Hollywood, CA: Newcastle Publishing Co., 1974, and John Anthony West, *Serpent in the Sky: The High Wisdom of Ancient Egypt,* Wheaton, IL: Theosophical Publishing House, 1993, chapter one.

3. *Chakra* is a Sanskrit word meaning "wheel." It is used to name the vortices of energy that help constitute the human field.

4. By Diane Kennedy Pike, New York: Riverhead Books, 1997.

5. www.kinfonet.org

6. Lutyens was quoting Jiddu Krishnamurti from *Freedom from the Known,* San Francisco: Harper San Francisco, 1975.

7. Quoted on the website: www.sriaurobindosociety.or.in/sriauro/aurolife.htm

8. The Mother (Mirra Alfassa), Sri Aurobindo's collaborator in Pondicherry, India, said these words when summarizing Sri Aurobindo's message, as given on the website cited above.

## Works Cited
The New English Bible.
The Krishnamurti website: www.kinfonet.org
Lutyens, Mary. *Krishnamurti: The Years of Fulfilment.* New York: Farrar, Straus, Giroux, 1983.
Merrell-Wolff, Franklin. *Pathways through to Space.* New York: The Julian Press, 1983.
Nisargadatta Maharaj. *I Am That.* Durham, NC: Acorn Press, 1973.
Prabhavananda, Swami. *The Spiritual Heritage of India.* Hollywood: Vedanta Press, 1979. Foreword by Huston Smith.

# THE PATH OF SELF-MASTERY
## BECOMING a CO-CREATOR in the WORLD

What we are not conscious of, controls us.
What we are conscious of, we can control.
— *Vitvan*

People who walk this pathway tend to see *themselves* as their greatest challenge and their greatest opportunity. They feel that to master their own functioning will be their primary contribution to the world.

The Path of Self-Mastery will serve you well if you believe that you have the power within you to change your self-expression. If you believe that there is untapped potential within you that you can learn to develop and bring forth, this Path may be yours. If you are willing to examine yourself — the way your body works, the way you feel, the way you think, what motivates you, what values you hold — and to make conscious choices about what you want to change, then you will find guidance here. If you believe that you are more than just a body and personality, that there are other facets of you that are beyond our usual forms of self-expression, and that there are powers available to you that cannot be understood by the rational mind, then pursuing Self-Mastery will enable you to confirm your convictions.

The Path of Self-Mastery is reflected on the secular level in our Western culture in the science of psychology. It is relatively new in our culture, which has been focused primarily on the Paths of Devotion and Action. Their influence has led to an attitude that if you have personal problems, you should take them to God in prayer or get busy serving others and forget yourself. The values of the Judeo-Christian culture have also led to a judgment that those who study themselves are self-centered in the sense of putting self first and God and others second.

Consequently, the Path of Self-Mastery in both Judaism and Christianity was confined to secret societies and esoteric schools for nearly two millennia. It was only in the twentieth century that esoteric teachings began to be brought out into the open.

In India the science of Yoga, which is the most fully developed presentation of the Pathway of Self-Mastery, has been widely available for more than two thousand years. It has been preserved by Yoga Masters who have passed on their wisdom and their techniques directly to their students.

Have you felt that mainline Judaism and Christianity are focused on serving God and others to the detriment or denial of the Self? Or have you accepted the teachings as valid, but kept asking yourself "how?" *How* can I Love God with all my heart and soul and mind? *How* can I devote myself to the selfless service of others when I have needs of my own? *How* can I try to improve the world around me when I am aware of so much in myself that needs to be changed and perfected? If so, then this Pathway may well be yours.

If you have been attracted to branches of Christianity such as Christian Science and Religious Science, to esoteric Christian teachings, to the Jewish Qabalah, to one or more forms of Yoga, or to occult teachings of various kinds, then most probably you will find that the Path of Self-Mastery will serve you well as you undertake your individual journey Home.

If on the other hand, you have been impatient with the self-help movement of the final thirty years of the twentieth century, feeling that it places self at the center instead of God, then you may find that the Pathway of Devotion serves you better. Or if you consider self-reflection and meditation an irresponsible escape from a world in which so much needs *doing,* you will want to consider the Path of Action. If you find psychology too small a focus, tending to offer shallow answers to large questions and to delude people into thinking that they are changing themselves when they are only tinkering with superficial behaviors, then you will undoubtedly find more satisfaction in the Pathway of Contemplation.

If you think this is probably *not* your Pathway, you may want to turn now to another chapter. If you do that, I encourage you to come back to this chapter later so that you can better understand others. The Path of Self-Mastery is coming into greater prominence in the West through the influence of psychology and Yoga. As problems increase, such as overt violence, the collapse of traditional family structures and educational systems, and the increase of heavy pressures and stresses in fast-paced work environments, many of those ready to pursue spiritual answers will turn to the Pathway of Self-Mastery. You will want to understand the nature of their Path so that you can appreciate the contribution they can make to you and to the world around you.

## FIRST STEPS ON THE PATH

The Pathway of Self-Mastery is based on the premise that all knowledge is based on experience and that no one can be genuinely spiritual until she has had the same experiences upon which the great religions are based. The Path of Self-Mastery is the science that teaches how to get those experiences. It is based on observing inner states and learning to concentrate the powers of the mind so that it can reflect on itself and know its own nature.

Those who walk this Pathway view the individual as a microcosm of the Whole. They understand the individual self to be a holographic fragment of the One Self out of which everything emerged. They believe that by coming to know the Self, they can learn all the laws and principles that are fundamental to cosmos. Thus the quest for Self-Mastery is a quest to become a conscious co-creator within the realm of manifestation.

In the beginning, you may not have such high aspirations. You may long for a much more basic understanding of yourself and the laws at work within you so that you can improve your life. Whether or not you aspire to mastery, you will want to begin with some basic steps.

### Step One:

Begin with self-observation. What works and

what doesn't work in your life? Start a journal in which to make notes of your observations. Your journal can be handwritten or computer-based. It can even be tape-recorded if you will take the time to go back and listen to what you have recorded.

Your observations should encompass four aspects of your life:

**The Physical:** Are you happy with the state of your physical body? Are you healthy, strong, agile, flexible, and able to express freely through your body? If not, what habits need to change? What healing do you need to effect? What new ways of eating do you need to establish? What new exercise regimes would serve you? Do you need to free yourself from any addictions?

**The Emotional:** Are you satisfied with your personal life? Do your relationships with family, friends, and significant others, partner, or spouse meet your needs for intimacy, love, security, pleasure, and caring? If not, what seems missing for you? What do you not know how to do? What do you long for? What do you regret? What more do you wish you could have or give? What do you need? Do you recognize patterns of co-dependency? Are you able to identify and express your feelings? Do you sometimes/often lose control emotionally? If so, under what circumstances? Do your emotions seem to rule your life?

**The Mental:** Do you feel mentally stimulated in your life? Are you growing and learning daily? How do you use your mind throughout the day? Do you worry a lot or obsess over things? Do you spend a lot of time thinking about other people and wondering what they think of you? Do you spend too much time reviewing things from the past? Do you dwell on mistakes you have made? How much time do you spend planning the future? Do you read books that are mentally challenging? Do you study and take courses that help you to develop mentally? Do you use your thinking as a tool or do your thoughts run rampant, distracting you from what is happening in the moment and often keeping you awake at night?

**The Spiritual:** Do you have a conscious spiritual life? Do you know how to listen to your inner voice of wisdom? Do you follow your intuition? Do you honor what you know by remaining true to it in word and deed? Do you know the Presence within? Do you have a strong will and know how to direct it? Are you able to quiet your body, feelings and mind so that you can experience the silence within? Do you take time each day for quiet study and reflection?

The intent of these observations is to gather as much information as you can about your present state of development. The notes you take will provide the foundation for your spiritual program as described in step two.

**Step Two:**
Outline a plan for your next growth steps. Using the observations you made under step one, identify what most needs your attention in each area: physical, emotional, mental, and spiritual. Decide on one course of action in relation to each of the four priorities you have identified.

When I first stepped onto this Pathway in my early thirties, I began by spending from one-half hour to two hours each morning in my spiritual practices. I followed the two-year lesson series developed by Swami Yogananda, an exemplar of this Path of Self-Mastery, and distributed by the Self-Realization Fellowship in Los Angeles.[1] Those lessons included exercises for charging the body with energy, breath work, and instructions in meditation.

I soon became aware that I needed to cleanse myself of old resentments. (See page 38 above for my description of the process I did.)

I learned to tone,[2] which is a way to use your voice for healing. And I began to study Yoga and other Eastern philosophies, a study that I continue to this day.

Your program will depend on what you observe that needs alignment in the way you live your life.

Pursue these plans of action until you begin to see change in the way you feel, think, and act, and until you come to some new perceptions.


## Step Three:

This step can be taken while you are working on step two. In fact, it may be an important part of one or more of your plans of action under step two.

Join at least one group where you can share your growth with others. This needs to be a group or groups in which you will receive feedback from others about how you are doing so that you do not fool yourself into thinking you are changing when you are not.

There are many kinds of groups available. You might find a Twelve-Step program that will help you to overcome an addiction or deal with a relational difficulty. Perhaps you will join a therapy group or go into couple's counseling. You might go to personal growth workshops or take a class in which there is active practice of personal growth strategies and techniques. Perhaps you will join a health club and work with a personal trainer on your physical program. You might take training in communication skills, stress management, or mind control. Perhaps you will join a spiritual study group or growth program.

The most important thing is to put yourself in a context where you can receive direct feedback on how you are doing in your personal growth program. Without the mirror-reflection that others provide, we often do not perceive ourselves clearly or accurately.

### Step Four:

Repeat step number two whenever you feel you have made enough progress on one course of action to take on the next challenge with regard to the physical, emotional, mental, and/or spiritual areas of your life.

### Step Five:

Study psychology. Popular self-help books may prove sufficient. What you want is a basic understanding of how the personality develops and what stumbling blocks commonly appear as you grow.

In the early stages of walking the Path of Self-Mastery I read nearly every new self-help book that came along. I found many of them to be very useful. I also attended classes and groups in which I could learn how I functioned in my relationships with others.

### Step Six:

When you feel you have acquired a basic understanding of yourself according to secular psychology, begin to study the Wisdom Teachings in one tradition or another so that you stretch your understanding of yourself into the more subtle realms of the psyche and spirit. You might study the teachings of Vitvan (the School of the Natural Order), Gurdjieff and his disciples (for example, Ouspensky and Bennett), Yogananda (the Self-Realization Fellowship), Rudolf Steiner (Anthroposophy), Alice Bailey (the Arcane School), or any number of other presentations of the Wisdom.[3] If you have access to someone who has received the Qabalah by oral transmission, you could benefit greatly from study with him. Any study of the Qabalah will contribute to your wider understanding of your place in the universe and how you reflect the Whole.[4]

This study of the Wisdom Teachings will continue for the rest of your life if you stay on this Pathway. I was first introduced to Yoga as a philosophy through Paramahansa Yogananda's *Autobiography of a Yogi*.[5] I began my study under the guidance of the Self-Realization Fellowship[6] for the first two years I walked this Path. During that time I was introduced to Vitvan, an American master of the Wisdom.[7] He became my primary teacher in 1973 and remains in that position to this day.

You will find that you will respond positively to some teachers and writings and not to others. Trust your responses. You will be guided by your own preferences to the presentations of the Wisdom that will serve you best.

### Step Seven:
Begin to learn to meditate. You may want to start with a simple five-minutes each morning in which you

sit quietly, breathe deeply, and relax in the silence. As you feel ready, you will want to expand that quiet time and to learn some techniques that will help you to go deeper in your practice of meditation. You could take a class or read some books.

I had already developed a regular morning discipline of study and prayer before stepping on the Path of Self-Mastery. I found it easy, then, to begin to meditate as I followed Yogananda's instruction. I also found a group with whom I sat in meditation once a week, and that was a great help to me. Depending on where you are in your own spiritual practices, you will find your way to meditation training and/or practice.

If you find these initial steps on the Path of Self-Mastery to be deeply satisfying as well as challenging, then you may well have found your most natural Path to Union. Walking this Pathway takes a lot of self-initiation, self-reflection, and self-discipline. You must learn to Love and trust yourself, for you are your own laboratory for experimentation and learning.

If you have a deep desire to know yourself and to understand how the power of the One Self works within you, then this Pathway will serve you well. If you long to be able to consciously channel and direct the creative force as it moves in you and through you, then you are ready to undertake more rigorous disciplines on this Path.


## MAKING A COMMITMENT

If you feel quite certain that you belong on the Path of Self-Mastery, you will want to make a commitment within yourself to follow the sort of disciplines that have served others along this way. You make this commitment to yourself. You will begin by getting to know yourself as a means of knowing the One Self. When you are able to function more consciously as an individualized expression of the One Self, you will become a more perfect reflection and expression of the power and potential that lies within you.

Life is a laboratory for you. Wherever you are, whatever you are doing, you are seeking to direct the power that flows through you so that everything you do and say is an expression of your conscious intention. No relationship or experience is irrelevant for you, for each is an opportunity to practice Self-Mastery. You seize every opportunity to know yourself better and to make conscious choices about your internal and external responses. Each life situation gives you evidence of the degree of your Self-Mastery and of the areas in which you need more knowledge and more development.

Mirra Alfassa (1878 - 1973), better known as "The Mother" of the Aurobindo Ashram in Pondicherry, India, was an outstanding exemplar of this Pathway in the twentieth century. According to her biography provided on the Sri Aurobindo Society website, she wrote that between the ages of 11 and 13 she already knew her purpose in life.

> A series of psychic and spiritual experiences revealed to me not only the existence of God but man's possibility of uniting with Him, of realizing Him integrally in consciousness and action. Of manifesting Him upon earth in a life Divine. (Website.)

To manifest God upon earth in a life Divine, as she called it, is a very large purpose that expresses what those who seek Self-Mastery are really asking of themselves. For that reason this Path demands enormous self-discipline. If your will is not well developed, you will need to have tremendous patience with yourself.

As you undertake new practices, don't be discouraged if you fail to sustain them. Rather, keep observing yourself. And when you notice that you have become lax in your disciplines, simply take a new breath and pick up where you left off. Don't waste time in self-recrimination and regret. There is no such thing as failure in consciousness work. When you become conscious that you are not practicing, you have taken a step in self-knowledge. Acknowledge what you see and take action on it. Then you will continue to grow in your ability to direct yourself along your chosen course.

To go deeper into your walk on the Path of Self-Mastery you will need to approach the objective world, what your senses register as external to you, as a lower frequency reflection of the subjective, or internal world that seems inaccessible to the senses.[8] On this Pathway you begin with the internal world, studying the nature of finer frequency energies. Through that study you will learn how to control and direct both internal and external forces.

## Cleanse Your Psyche

You will need to undergo a rigorous cleansing of the psyche, which is your internal space. You need to eradicate any tendency within you to inflict injury on anyone, by thought, word or deed. In order to do this work you must be willing to be painfully honest with yourself. You will need to uncover and transform subtle urges that other people might not even be able to detect in you.

Observe yourself throughout the day in your interactions, not only with other people, but also with other living creatures. Do you automatically step on spiders? Do you squash gnats and small bugs just because they are there? Do you slap people on the back so hard that they spontaneously recoil? Do you spank or slap your children?

Listen to yourself when you speak. Do you lash out in anger? Do you use sarcasm instead of stating a feeling or offering an opinion directly? Do you criticize harshly? Do you call people names or use demeaning humor?

Observe your thoughts. Are you silently critical of others and of yourself? Do you rehearse conversations in which you will tell others off or put them down? Do you harbor resentments based on past events?

Have you been dishonest in your relationships? Have you taken what did not belong to you, in whatever form? Have you used other persons for your own gain or for the satisfaction of your own desires? Have you refused to receive the blessing of others' gifts to you of their love, their talents, and their wisdom?

In these and other ways that you will discover, you may be sending forth energy that is meant to wound others and to squelch the Life Force. To walk the Path of Self-Mastery, you must eradicate all such behaviors along with the impulses behind them, however innocuous they might seem to others and however much pleasure or power you may have derived from them in the past. You will come to understand that energy that is harmful to others is self-destructive as well, for there is only one Self. You cannot move toward Oneness when you are rejecting and harming other facets of that One with whom you seek to unite.

When I wanted to eradicate all urges to do violence to others, I became a vegetarian. This meant that each time I ate I was reminded of my commitment to live nonviolently. By not eating meat, I did not participate in the slaughter of animals. I also redirected the energy of my impulses to be critical of others, to judge others, and to inflict harm. I practiced finding something I could praise or appreciate about everyone that came into my consciousness. I also remember canceling the pest control service for my home and learning to capture insects and release them outdoors instead of killing them.

The only truly effective way to change behaviors that inflict harm on others is to redirect the energy into expressions of unconditional Love. You must truly *want* to transmute the negativity and violence first. Then you will be able to learn to lift the energy into the Heart. If your desire to become a conscious expression of your full potential is strong enough, you will be willing to sacrifice whatever pleasure you derived in the past from those destructive skills and habits in order to know the higher pleasure of the Heart, namely joy. Therefore, you will want to focus on opening your Heart Center and directing Love energy consciously to all with whom you interact in your inner and outer worlds.

When I discovered the Love Principles,[9] soon after stepping onto the Path of Self-Mastery, I immediately adopted them as my way of transforming all harmful impulses into expressions of Unconditional Love. They continue to be central to my practice.

Unconditional Love provides a foundation for your journey on the road to Self-Mastery. Learning to Love without any impulse to violence or harm could take you a lifetime or two. But even as you are cleansing your psyche, you will undertake other facets of your work, since each enhances the others. Moreover, at every step of your process of unfolding into consciousness of the One, you will discover ever more subtle energies that need to be transmuted, until the psyche is such a clear reflection of higher frequencies energies that it dissolves into Oneness with them.

## Cleanse Your Body

On the Pathway of Self-Mastery the body is a major instrument for the expression of the Will, for the Will is buried in the body until we raise it into our consciousness. The Will of the One Self is being done through the unconscious-to-us processes at work in our bodies. However, desires and preferences of the *psyche* often establish habit patterns that impede the expression of the Will. Consequently, it is very important that you cleanse your body and prepare it to respond to and transmit not only the innate impulses of the One Self but also the higher frequency energies of the creative force brought into conscious awareness.

You will want to free yourself of any addictions to food or drink. You may want to practice fasting to cleanse your body of toxins from the past. And you will want to nourish your body from this day forward with natural food and water that are not full of preservatives, chemical additives, hormones, etc. Healthy food and water are the foundation for your work in the body.

When I became a vegetarian, I took time to learn about how to feed my body with natural foods in order to keep it healthy. I also undertook regular water fasts to cleanse my body of toxins. These practices have been integrated into my daily living.

You will want to practice regular stretches and exercises that keep your body limber and aligned. Hatha Yoga was specifically designed for this. The various postures that you learn in Hatha Yoga not only align the body but also help to purify your nerves so that they can register and transmit higher frequency energies. Hatha Yoga teachers are quite widely available these days throughout the West as well as in India. You will advance more quickly along your Path of Self-Mastery if you study with a fine Yoga teacher.

I have been walking this Path for over thirty years now. I continue to do forty minutes of stretches every morning before going out for my physical exercise, which is either an hour of tennis or a four-mile walk. I find these disciplines essential to my functioning on all levels. You will develop your own program to sustain your physical flexibility, stability, strength, and endurance, and your adherence to that program will be vital to your development on other levels.

Other approaches to mastery of functioning through the body will also serve you well. Tai Chi and other martial arts, dance, and whole-body sports will all help you to function consciously in the body.

## Control Your Breath

Perhaps the most important skill you will develop as you move toward Self-Mastery is to control your breath.  Breathing is an autonomic function of the body. The body stops breathing only if it is deprived of oxygen. However, unlike other autonomic functions, breathing can be taken over by conscious volition. A master yogi, for example, can stop his physical breath for days at a time if he wishes. This skill has been tested and verified by Western scientists under strictly controlled circumstances.

Though you may have no interest in learning to stop your breath for long periods of time, it is important for you to know that the breath gives you conscious access to unconscious functions such as your heart rate, your nervous system, your brain, and the Life Force itself. By controlling the breath you can control these other functions that would otherwise be out of your conscious purview.

There is an entire branch of the science of Yoga dedicated to breath control. It is called *pranayama*.[10] *Prana* is the Sanskrit word for life force, and *yama* means self-restraint. To learn to control prana, you begin with what you know most intimately: namely, your breath.

You will want at the least to learn some of the basic exercises that have been taught for centuries by Yoga masters. These exercises set forces in motion in the body that can only be activated through systematic practice at least twice a day, in the morning and in the evening.

Here is an example of a basic exercise for restraining prana:

1. Sit with your spine erect either on a chair or cross-legged on the floor.
2. Remember that you are an inherent part of cosmos.
3. Breathe into your desire for knowledge and Light and release that desire as a prayer.

4. Visualize your physical body as firm, strong, and healthy.
5. Breathe in to the count of four; hold the breath for the count of two; breathe out for the count of four; hold the breath for the count of two.

This exercise will help you to begin to establish rhythmic breathing as your regular way of breathing throughout the day. Rhythmic breathing brings order and balance to your body by training all the molecules of the body to move in the same direction and thus to function harmoniously. When the breath flow is irregular and unbalanced it is more difficult for the organs of the body to stay healthy.

Gradually, as you practice rhythmic breathing you will be able to lengthen the breath. As you do so, you will continue to hold the breath for half of the count between inhale and exhale. If you inhale for eight counts, you will hold for four, then exhale for eight, and hold for four, etc.

The deeper the breath, the more fully you will charge the molecules of the body with Life Force. The energy in the molecules is then transformed into nerve currents that bring all of the activities of the body into rhythmic resonance. This makes it possible for you, after long practice, to direct the body through the conscious exercise of will.

Rhythmic breathing is only the beginning of the practice of breath control. If you study *pranayama* with a teacher or learn more of the many patterns of breathing that are part of that science, you will increase your own ability to control the breath and thus to express yourself consciously by directing the different frequencies of energy that move through your field.

When I have the opportunity to work with groups, I usually tell them that if I could teach them only one thing, it would be to breathe consciously. I find it the most important of all the consciousness tools I know.

### Direct Energy

As you develop the ability to control your breathing, you will become aware that you can direct the energies coursing through your field by aligning your attention and your will with your breathing. The flow of energy will follow your attention.

For example, if you focus on your left hand and then consciously inhale, on the exhale the flow of energy to your left hand will increase dramatically. If you continue to hold the focus and to breathe consciously, you will first experience an increase of heat in your hand. Then you may see the color change. Then you may have the sensation that the hand is swelling, though the actual size will not change. You may feel prickly sensations or static as if an electrical current were running through your hand. If you were to place that hand next to, but not touching, your left cheek, you would be able to feel the strength of the energy flow.

This simple example illustrates the basic principle: you can direct the flow of energy by focusing your attention and aligning your breathing with your intention to send energy to or through a given space in your own field or in someone else's. Since energy is the capacity for action, you will be able to function effectively in many ways previously not available to you once you learn this skill.

### Identify the Seven Energy Centers

There are many descriptions of the human energy field, but perhaps the simplest and most universally accepted is that provided by the Eastern philosophies. Those philosophies describe seven streams of force that are received and regulated by seven centers. Each energy center, called a *chakra* (which means "wheel" in Sanskrit), governs a spectrum of energy wavelengths.

The seven centers are the Sacral or Root Chakra, associated with the base of the spine; the Generative Chakra, associated with the reproductive organs; the Solar Plexus Chakra, associated with the digestive organs; the Heart Chakra, associated with all circulatory systems; the Throat Chakra, associated with the ears, mouth and throat; the Third Eye or Brow Chakra, associated with the eyes and head; and the Crown Chakra, associated with the crown of the head and the area above the crown. You can learn to discriminate between the energies regulated by each of the chakras.

In the beginning, you will associate the energies with the activities that are empowered by them. For example, you will associate the Solar Plexus with emotions (feelings), the Throat Chakra with thinking and speaking, the Generative Chakra with movement and expression through the body, and the Heart Center with unconditional Love and acts of generosity.

As you practice holding your attention on the area of the body associated with each chakra and breathing in and out through that center, you will learn to experience the *energy* behind those activities. Perhaps in the beginning you will notice a physical sensation associated with activity in that center. But eventually you will be able to identify the *qualities* of the energy in each center.

There is a large literature available today on the energy centers.[11] Reading about them will familiarize you with some of the experiences associated with each. However, reading can never be a substitute for coming to know the energy of each center through your own experience. This is why practicing the coordination of your breathing with your attention focused on the centers is so important.

### Direct Energy through the Chakras

Once you have practiced breathing through the energy centers enough to recognize characteristics of each band of wave frequencies, you will want to begin to direct the energy. You can practice during your quiet time each morning. For example, you can breath energy into the Generative Chakra and then, on the exhale, lift that energy up into the Solar Plexus. Then breathe into the Solar Plexus and on the exhale direct the force up into the Heart Center. Continue until you lift the force to the Crown Center and release it there.

This practice will serve you in your daily life when, in ordinary interactions or activities, you register energy in a given center and want to transform it by lifting it to a higher frequency. You will learn to recognize that living is all about the transformation of energy, and that as one who is learning to live more consciously, you will want to assume greater and greater responsibility for transforming energies through the exercise of will. When you lift energies from one center to another, you effect a transformation within your own field, and that change in turn affects all those with whom you interact.

I remember the time my partner and I were confronted by a friend and his lawyer. We had entered into an agreement with this friend to publish some of his artwork if we were able to raise the money to do so. After making an effort to raise funds, we told him we could not go ahead with the publishing. His lawyer said he was going to take us to court to recover the "damages" our friend had suffered because we were backing out of the project.

The two of us were completely stunned by this announcement. I remember noticing that I was registering the energy of the lawyer in my Throat Chakra and our friend's energy in the Solar Plexus. I turned my attention to my breathing and pulled the energy from both of those chakras into my Heart Center. I then breathed out Love to our friend and his lawyer.

During the next two hours, as we shared back and forth about what had transpired, I continued to stay centered in my Heart. When I had an opportunity, I said, in a calm but forceful voice, "There is no way I am going to court." Eventually the lawyer left, saying he was sure the three of us could work out our differences. Then our friend said, "I know that you had only the best intentions and did everything you did out of Love. I think we can just let this all go and move forward in Love."

Using the breath to transform my own energy not only enabled me to function consciously and to remain centered, it also had an effect on our friend and his lawyer. There was no doubt about that, since the energy of confrontation dissolved and our friend's Heart opened to us again.

## Express Clearly and Powerfully

You will also learn to express yourself more clearly and powerfully by coordinating your attention and breath with your chosen activities throughout the day. If you are reading a book and want to understand what you are reading, for example, it will help if you breathe into the Throat Chakra, where you are registering the thoughts, and lift the energy to the Third Eye Center, where you will understand more clearly. If you are in a conversation with someone who is sharing deep feelings, you will want to breathe into the Solar Plexus so that the speaker feels heard. If you then lift those forces into your Heart Center, you will be able to release them as unconditional Love. In that way the residue of the other person's feelings will not remain in your field.

This use of the breath to direct and transform energy will be one of the most powerful skills you will develop as you walk the Path of Self-Mastery.

## Train Your Mind

If you have spent time observing your mind, you will be familiar with the way it functions when you are not consciously directing it. Perhaps it simply wanders off in vague reveries of which you have no memory when you return to the present moment. Or your mind may talk to you, running commentary on what you are doing or not doing. Or does your mind watch others and assess how they are living their lives, forming opinions and judgments about them? Perhaps your mind worries, conjuring up images of disaster, pain and hardship for your future or the future of others. Or your mind may make lists of things to do, or rehearse conversations it thinks you ought to have with people. Whatever your mind's proclivity, it is time now for you to take control of it.

Training the mind is analogous to training a dog. You must approach your mind in the full confidence that you are the "master" and that the mind *will* obey if you are persistent and consistent with it. Your purpose is to teach the mind to stay focused in the here/now moment of your awareness. This is something like teaching a dog to heel. When you are walking with your dog you want it to walk along beside you, not to dash off in all directions chasing cats or rabbits or sniffing bushes. It is the same with the mind. Whatever activity you are engaged in, you want the mind to stay with you, not to wander off into daydreams, or to occupy itself with thoughts regarding the past or future, or to reflect on the activities of others. You want it to be focused in the present so that it can serve you whenever you need it.

After over thirty years of disciplining my mind, it rarely gets out of my control anymore. I am able to hold it focused throughout the day as I move from task to task, and from interaction to interaction. And at the end of the day, it is easy to fall off to sleep without having to struggle to make my mind settle down. And most important, my mind serves me extremely well throughout the day. When I need important information, I send the mind to retrieve it, much like you might send your dog to retrieve the morning paper. Depending on how deep the information has been buried in the archives of my memory, the mind brings me the information almost immediately or after some time has passed. But it rarely fails to find the data I need.

You will have similar satisfaction if you are consistent and persistent in training your mind, Once you have trained it, it will be able to capture the reflection of material you bring in from higher frequencies, received through intuition and direct perception.


## Detach the Mind from the Senses

Teach your mind to register sensory data without attaching labels or images to it. For example, as you sit quietly, you will notice sounds in the environment around you and perhaps even within your own body. Practice hearing the sound without thinking "that's a bird" or "the furnace just came on" or "the neighbor is using his drill" or "there must be an accident on the corner." Instead, focus on the sensation itself. How does the sound *feel* as you register it? Do not let your mind wander to any images associated with the sound. Keep it focused on the sound itself.

Do the same with the other senses. The most difficult will be the sense of sight, because as soon as you open your eyes you will see images. That is how our objective consciousness registers what we see. But you can practice not allowing any labels or thoughts to form in the mind as you register light and color and shapes and textures. You can practice this by setting an object in front of you and simply looking at it, without thought. Try to experience what it "feels" like to see.

As you discipline the mind not to automatically form images or give labels to sensory data, you will find that you are gaining control over it. When we function unconsciously, our minds automatically respond to the stimuli registered by the five senses. Images are awakened and thinking begins without our even noticing. When you teach the mind to remain still while you attend to sensory data you have, in effect, taught it to obey your own voice, the voice of its master.

This exercise brings me such great joy as I practice it each morning and from time to time throughout the day. I feel attuned to the energy world around me and my whole field resonates with the harmony of the spheres.

## Learn to Concentrate

In today's culture, concentration on a single spot or object is very difficult. We are barraged daily with flashing images and rapidly moving objects. Our eyes are not used to sustaining a focus for more than fractions of a second. In addition, our environment is flooded with dissonant and jarring sounds that contribute to the sensation of constant motion and change. In response to this constantly changing visual and auditory stimulation, our minds are persistently restless and distracted.

Once you have begun to detach the functioning of the mind from sensory data, you will be able to practice concentration. Begin by setting an object before you and holding your attention on the object without thinking about it. This is an extension of the practice of detaching the mind from sensory data. You are seeing the object, but not labeling it or thinking about it. You might choose to concentrate on a mandala, or a burning candle, or a favorite symbol.

The purpose of this kind of concentration is to break out of objective thinking, which is to perceive the world as separate from us, and to perceive instead the energy Reality as it is. Thus, as you concentrate, you will want to have no expectations about what will happen. You may suddenly break through to a new perception, understanding, or experience that changes the way you understand yourself and the world around you.

Vivekananda was a Yoga master from India who came to this country in the early part of the 20th century to teach the science of Yoga to those Westerners who were eager for such knowledge.[12]   He writes:

> The yogis say that if the mind is concentrated on the tip of the nose, after a few days one begins to smell wonderful perfumes. If it is concentrated on the root of the tongue, one begins to hear sounds; if on the tip of the tongue, one begins to taste wonderful flavors; if on the middle of the tongue, one feels as if one were coming in contact with some object. If one concentrates the mind on the palate one begins to see strange things. (132-133)

The point is that through concentrating the mind, we discover that no objects are separate from self and solid, including our own bodies. Instead, we find that when we are able to penetrate through apparent objects, we have an experience of what the object represents on a functional level, as did the yogis in Vivekananda's example. The tip of the tongue represents the function of tasting, the middle of the tongue represents kinesthetic sensing, and the root of the tongue represents hearing. Or by focusing on apparent objects we might awaken new insights and understandings of the world around us and of ourselves.

Something else happens through the exercise of

concentration. Your mind begins to extend to the periphery of your mental field. When this happens, your individualizing field of energy is stimulated to further development. New faculties of consciousness begin to awaken and your field becomes better organized and more coordinated in its functioning. You may not be immediately aware of these changes, but they will be occurring nevertheless, furthering your growth toward Union with the One Self.

The key to concentration is to hold the mind fixed on certain points and not to let it stray by thinking *about* anything. I find I need to practice this daily in order to keep the ability sharp.

### Learn to Meditate

When the mind has been trained to concentrate by remaining fixed on a certain internal point or external object, a new power is awakened in it. It is as if an unbroken current of energy flows from within the mind towards the object of attention.

Sit up straight and concentrate on the tip of your nose. Holding that focus of your attention, allow an image of your choosing to form in your mind. For example, you might imagine that in front of you there lies a vast body of water, so large that you cannot see the shores. The water is utterly still, causing it to reflect the perfectly clear blue sky above. You watch the lake in your mind's eye, realizing that it is like the mirror of your mind. You hold the image of the lake and the awareness that the mind is like the lake and you meditate on that. *You do not think about it.* Instead, you hold your attention focused on it until you can begin to feel the streaming of your mental powers into the image. Deep insights will begin to come in response.

Or, with your eyes closed and your eyes focused on a spot just between your eyebrows, hold a question you long to have answered, such as "what is wanted of me?" or "how shall I proceed?" *Do not think about the question.* Instead, hold the question in your consciousness as if you were looking at it with your eyes. Concentrate on it. In time, you will feel your mind streaming out to the question, as if penetrating it with power from within you. An answer will come without any effort on your part.

I find this essential to receiving inner guidance, especially at important turning points in my life. When my mind gets busy thinking about things, it is like being in an inner storm. I cannot register finer frequencies at all. I cannot stand in the stillness.

But when I can meditate on a question, the answer comes with directness and simplicity. It is a wonderful gift. I remember the time a friend was diagnosed with uterine cancer. I was so disturbed by the news that I went into my meditation room and sat down. I focused on the question "What is cancer?" and I set my intention not to get up until I got an answer. It was not long until understanding began to pour in. To this day I am comforted by what was given in response to that question. Although it would be a sidetrack to share the insight here,  I have shared it with many over the years.

This deep penetration into the object of your concentration is what is called meditation. It is a profoundly nourishing activity that enables you to contact higher frequency energies such as expanded consciousness and the creative forces. These higher frequency energies will eventually enable you to register the energy of unity.

## Experience Union

After years of practice with concentration and meditation, you may experience Union with the One Self. As you are meditating, you will suddenly find that your whole self is merging with the object of your concentration. Then the single focus expands until it encompasses all.

Here is an example of such an experience. Paramahansa Yogananda, another yogic ambassador from India during the first half of the twentieth century, wrote in his *Autobiography of a Yogi*:

> Soul and mind instantly lost their physical bondage and streamed out like a fluid piercing light from my every pore. . . . My sense of identity was no longer narrowly confined to a body but embraced the circumambient atoms. People on distant streets seemed to be moving gently over my own remote periphery. . . . My ordinary frontal vision was now changed to a vast spherical sight, simultaneously all-perceptive . . . until all melted into a luminescent sea; even as sugar crystals, thrown into a glass of water, dissolve after being shaken. . . . An oceanic joy broke upon calm endless shores of my soul. The Spirit of God, I realized, is exhaustless Bliss; His body is countless tissues of light. . . . The Entire cosmos, gently luminous, like a city seen afar at night, glimmered within the infinitude of my being. . . . Irradiating splendor issued from my nucleus to every part of the universal structure. . . . The creative voice of God I heard resounding as Aum, the vibration of the Cosmic Motor. (149-150)

Of course each experience of Union is unique, but paradoxically the perceptions and confirmations of the nature of Reality are universal. Yogananda's words provide one glimpse of what awaits you if you are faithful in your practice of meditation.

## THE DANGERS

Perhaps the greatest danger on the Path of Self-Mastery is getting caught in the ego-state and pouring your energy into the development of a sense of yourself as separate rather than shifting your identity to the Real Self. If this happens, you will begin to feel that you, as a separate and unique individual, are "important" and that you know more than others or are superior to others. Should this happen, you will cease to walk the Path and will remain encased in the shell of ego.

It is essential to learn to discriminate between the ego and the Real Self so that when you direct your energies toward mastery you do not mistake the personality for the individualized Self. The more individualized you become, the clearer your perception will become that you are an integral part of the realization of the Whole. That is, you are like one cell of a large body. Your personal growth is not yours in some separate way. Everything you do contributes to and is an expression of the One Self.

I remember distinctly the narrow street I was walking through in Varanasi, India, on my first trip there in 1979. Varanasi is the "holy city" of the Hindus, and pilgrims crowded around me, pressing to get to the shrines they would visit. They carried flowers and sweets to offer as expressions of their devotion. An awareness rushed through my whole field and registered as a profound knowing: "I am not going anywhere without all these people."

In that moment my illusion that I was somehow

developing like a fruit without a branch, or a branch without a tree, fell away. I realized that I am an integral part of One Self, and just as each organ of my body contributes to the well being of the whole body and is an expression of the whole body, so I am integrated in the body of humanity. What I am becoming is an expression of the whole body, not some separate accomplishment of my ego.

These words of Martin Buber were intended to elucidate the teachings of Hassidism, or in the terms of this book, the Path of Devotion. They could apply, however, to any of the Pathways, and they are especially appropriate here, for one walking the Path of Self-Mastery:

> One need only ask one question: "What for?" What am I to choose my particular way for? What am I to unify my being for? The reply is: Not for my own sake. This is why the previous injunction was " to *begin* with oneself; to start from oneself, but not to aim at oneself; to comprehend oneself, but not to be preoccupied with oneself. (34-35)

The guidance of a teacher can be especially helpful in this regard to one walking this Path. By clearly pointing out when you slip into identification with the ego, which is only the embryonic expression of the Self you long to know, the teacher can help you not to deceive yourself.

When you walk the Path of Self-Mastery, certain powers may be awakened in you that can also be the occasion for you to stray from the Path. In the West these are usually called psychic powers; in the East they are called *siddhis.* These powers are numerous and any one or more of them might awaken in you. A few examples are the ability to read what is in the mind of another, to see future events before they transpire, to heal diseases and bodily deformities, to transform material substances, to materialize objects, to bilocate, and to levitate.

It is easy to become absorbed in the expression of these powers and to lose sight of your ultimate goal, which is Union with the Divine. In fact, if you identify with these powers, thinking they are "yours" in some personal sense, you can actually separate yourself in consciousness from the One with whom you set out to unite.

The Mother (see page 131 above) began to have such powers at a very early age. She wrote:

> When I was a child of about thirteen, for nearly a year every night as soon as I had gone to bed it seemed to me that I went out of my body and rose straight up above the house, then above the city, very high above. Then I used to see myself clad in a magnificent golden robe, much longer than myself; and as I rose higher, the robe would stretch, spreading out in a circle around me to form a kind of immense roof over the city. Then I would see men, women, children, old men, the sick, the unfortunate coming out from every side; they would gather under the outspread robe, begging for help, telling of their miseries, their suffering, their hardships. In reply, the robe, supple and alive, would extend towards each one of them individually, and as soon as they had touched it, they were comforted or healed, and went back into their bodies happier and stronger than they had come out of them. Nothing seemed more beautiful to me, nothing could make me happier; and all the activities of the day seemed dull and colorless and without any real life, beside this activity of the night which was the true life for me.[13]

It would have been easy for young Mirra to feel so special that she would not go further on the Path. She could have developed an inflated ego instead of realizing that the power that flowed through her in those nightly experiences is a universal and impersonal force. Fortunately, however, Mirra kept going along the Path toward Self-Mastery. She developed her talents for drawing and painting and became a gifted musician and an accomplished tennis player.

However, it was the call of the Spirit that was foremost in her life. Between the ages of 11 and 13 she had a series of psychic and spiritual experiences during her body's sleep. She also received a practical discipline for the fulfillment of her vision of manifesting God on earth in a life Divine, as she called it. Several teachers, some of whom she met afterwards on the physical plane, gave these experiences to her.

Because Mirra had so many psychic and spiritual experiences, she spent two years studying with a couple who were very advanced in the occult sciences. From them she learned to master the psychic realm without attaching importance to such powers. She knew that the psychic powers were just a proof that there are other forces than purely material ones.

By the time Mirra was thirty-four she knew that she had a large mission to accomplish in the realm of the transformation of energies. She devoted the rest of her life, until her death at age 95, to integrating that new consciousness into her own field and to guiding others in their spiritual development toward that same end. She became a powerful force of Love in the ashram she founded in Pondicherry, India. This she could not have done had she become distracted by the psychic powers that were so fully developed in her.

As you walk this Pathway and practice the disciplines associated with it, you must always remember that there is only One Self expressing through countless individualizing energy fields. As the powers of this One Self begin to express through you, you must not become personally identified with them, thinking that they make you special or unique in some way. Rather, you must offer gratitude for these signs that you are moving toward greater Union with the One, and you must stay focused on deepening your meditation toward that end.

Another danger of the Path of Self-Mastery is that you will grow impatient with the process of your unfoldment and become discouraged that you have not progressed as far as you had hoped. Or you may decide to settle for the gains you have made and slack off in your disciplines. If such impatience arises within you, it will be helpful to seek out the companionship of others walking this Path, or to seek the counsel of a teacher.

## SUMMARY

To summarize this presentation of the Path of Self-Mastery, we can say that this is the way of the practical scientist in the laboratory of life, whether as psychologist, teacher, or magician. The focus of one walking this Pathway is valued more highly in our culture today than it was a century ago. However, the powerful influence of Judaism and Christianity continue to fuel the judgment that there is something self-serving about those who seek to understand the process of the developing self. Consequently, you will find that people will suspect you of being selfish or self-centered and will wonder if you are actually contributing anything to the world around you when you walk this Path.

As you begin to walk this Pathway, you will be motivated by a desire to know yourself and to understand how Divine power works within you so that you will be able to consciously channel and direct that power. You study yourself in order to know the One Self more consciously and directly because you know yourself to be a microcosmic reflection of the original One. Eventually you begin to understand that everything you do and are serves the One Self.

It is your goal to attain Union with the One Self and to learn to sustain that Union in the midst of everyday life. You are aware that only by being able to function in full consciousness as an individualized being can you be a perfect reflection of the One Self. Then all you do will enhance the Whole.

You know that when you become fully conscious nothing will be out of your control. Consequently, you begin with where you are and learn to control the breath, which is already known to you. Through rhythmic breathing you seek to align all the molecules of the body to get them moving in the same direction. When all the movements of the body have become perfectly rhythmical, your body becomes a gigantic battery of will at your disposal.

As you continue your breath work, you purify the nerve currents and learn to control your thoughts. Utilizing a focused mind and conscious breathing, you learn to register energy consciously and to direct your life force with purpose and conscious intention.

The aim of all this is to release the power (called the *Kundalini* in Sanskrit) in the Sacral Center so that it can unite with the forces of the Crown Center. This makes it possible for the Life Force (*Prana*) and Consciousness to merge in one flow as the Creative Power in you. To be able to function as a conscious co-creator is to assume your place as one who has actualized your human potential. This is Self-Mastery, and with it comes the knowledge of the individualized Self as the One Self in manifestation.

---

1. Self-Realization Fellowship, 3880 San Rafael Avenue, Dept. 9W, Los Angeles, CA 90065-3298. Phone: 323-225-2471. Website: www.yogananda-srf.org

2. See *Toning,* by Laurel Elizabeth Keyes, Marina del Rey, CA: DeVorss & Co., 1973; *The Roar of Silence,* by Don G. Campbell, Wheaton: The Theosophical Publishing House, 1989; and *Healing Sounds: The Power of Harmonics,* by Jonathan Goldman, Rockport, MA: Element Books, 1992.

3. School of the Natural Order, P.O. Box 150, Baker, NV 89311. Phone: 775-234-7304. Website: www.sno.org; Self-Realization Fellowship, 3880 San Rafael Avenue, Dept. 9W, Los Angeles, CA 90065-3298. Phone: 323-225-2471. Website: www.yogananda-srf.org; Theosophical Society in America (and Quest Books), P.O. Box 270, Wheaton, IL 60189-0270. Phone: 630-668-1571, ext. 300, or Quest Books: 630-665-0130. E-mail: olcott@theosmail.net. Website: www.theosophical.org; The Arcane School, 120 Wall Street, 24th Floor, New York, NY 10005. Phone: 212-292-0707. E-mail: newyork@lucistrust.org. Website: www.lucistrust.org/arcane/. The Anthroposphic Press, PO Box 96, Herndon, VA 20172-0960. Phone: 1-800-856-8664. Fax: 1-800-277-9747. Website: service@anthropress.org. Also see website: www.steinercollege.org/rs.html.

4. The Society of the Inner Light, of which Dion Fortune was a member, is a Society for the study of Occultism, Mysticism, and Esoteric Psychology and the development of their practice. Its aims

are Christian and its methods are Western. For further details, write: The Secretariat, The Society of the Inner Light, 38 Steele's Road, London NW3 4RG England.

5. Los Angeles: Self-Realization Fellowship, 1969.

6. See note 1 above.

7. See Richard Satriano, *Vitvan: An American Master,* Baker, NV: School of the Natural Order, 1977.

8. See Pike, *Life As A Waking Dream.*

9. See Appendix One: The Gateway of the Heart.

10. See, for example, B. K. S. Iyengar's book *Light on Pranayama: The Yogic Art of Breathing,* with Introduction by Yehudi Menuhin, New York: Crossroad, 1981, for an extensive presentation of this science.

11. Some of my favorites are: Gurudev Shree Chitrabhanu, *The Psychology of Enlightenment: Meditations on the Seven Energy Centers,* New York: Dodd, Mead & Company, 1979; C. W. Leadbeater, *The Chakras,* Wheaton, IL: Quest Books, 1974; Shafica Karagulla, M.D. and Dora van Gelder Kunz, *The Chakras and the Human Energy Fields,* Wheaton, IL: Quest Books, 1989; Djwal Kul, *Intermediate Studies of the Human Aura,* Los Angeles: Summit University Press, 1976.

12. Vivekananda's books on the four yogic Paths to Union are classic presentations of the wisdom contained in Pantanjali's *Sutras.* See *Raja-Yoga, Bhakti-Yoga, Jnana-Yoga* and *Karma-Yoga,* all by Vivekananda and published by the Ramakrishna-Vivekananda Center in New York or the Vedanta Press in Los Angeles.

13 The Mother, *Prayers and Meditations,* as quoted on the Aurobindo Society website: www.sriaurobindosociety.org.in/mother/motherlf.htm

## Works Cited

Buber, Martin. *The Way of Man: According to the Teachings of Hasidism.* Chicago: A Cloister Press Book, 1951.

The Sri Aurobindo Society Web Site: www.sriaurobindosociety. org.in/mother/motherlf.htm

Vivekananda, Swami. *Raja-Yoga.* New York: Ramakrishna-Vivekananda Center, 1970.

Yogananda, Paramahansa. *Autobiography of a Yogi.* Los Angeles: Self-Realization Fellowship, 1969.

# CHOOSING A PATH

*Each soul is potentially divine. The goal is to manifest this divinity within by controlling nature, external and internal. Do this either by work, or worship, or psychic control, or philosophy – by one, or more, or all of these – and be free. This is the whole of religion. Doctrines, or dogmas, or rituals, or books, or temples, or forms, are but secondary details.*

— *Vivekananda*

A spiritual Pathway is not a religion. It is an individualized approach to the quest for meaning, for purpose, for a worthy cause or leader to which you can dedicate yourself, or for self-knowledge. Each Pathway has a specific focus and specific disciplines. Each tends to appeal to a different personality type or character structure. Each leads to the same end: an experience of oneness, or Union, that causes you to feel whole, free and at peace with yourself, the world, your destiny, and the Divine.

Because most of us are accustomed to think in terms of organized religions, you may not have been aware that there comes a time when humans are impelled by their own nature to find their own, individualized way as they unfold their further potential. It often comes as a feeling that you need to find the meaning or purpose of your own life, and it is often accompanied by the knowing, though you may not know how or why you know, that you must do this alone.

If you are an adventuresome person, but not reckless, you will probably do a lot of investigating before you set out alone to climb the metaphorical spiritual mountain. You may read books about mountain climbing. You may take some training. You will probably talk with other mountain climbers. You may even go on some excursions with groups until you become familiar with the challenges and dangers of mountain climbing. You will learn the techniques you need to know to make your solo climb safely and successfully. You will certainly research the mountain itself to inform yourself of the best approach for you to make, and to discover what provisions you will need for the climb. Finally, you will no doubt undertake your own program of training to get in shape, in top condition, for the concentrated effort ahead of you.

You could simply set out through the woods and thickets surrounding the spiritual foothills and find your own way to the metaphorical mountain, but the passage would likely be longer and far more arduous. Moreover, it would be easy to become disoriented and lose your way. You might encounter impassable obstacles and have to backtrack, and you might become discouraged or even injured along the way and give up. Consequently, the less experienced the mountain-climber, the more prudent it is to find a Pathway that has already been cut.

For this phase of the journey, you are a spiritual seeker. You are investigating, exploring, discovering, learning and practicing, not because you are a dilettante who is not committed to the big climb, but because you are preparing yourself. It is while you are seeking that you will identify which Pathway you want to climb. This will enable you to map out your journey, learn all you can about what to expect along the way, and practice the techniques that will serve you.

When the time is right, you will go to the mountain and begin your solo climb at a particular place and by a particular route. At that point you become a disciple, because you will have chosen your discipline.

On the lowlands of everyday living where religions are practiced, it would seem that the various approaches to Union are quite different one from the other. But once the ascent is begun, individual climbers will meet and cross the Pathways of others, and it will become more and more evident that all Paths lead to the same summit.


## The Nature of a Path

What, then, is a spiritual Pathway? It is a well-defined approach to Union with the Ultimate, characterized by particular disciplines, life-styles, interests, preferences and proclivities. It is not a doctrine *about* the trek. It is a description of the journey as made by others who have achieved Union and returned to tell about it. It is not a rationale designed to convince you that Union with the Divine is a good idea. Rather it is a series of signposts and training programs for those who are determined to pursue Union and are seeking help to find their way. A Pathway is not a conveyance that will carry you along, but it will offer way stations where you can enjoy the encouragement of companions on the journey.

You step onto a Pathway by making a conscious choice to devote yourself whole-heartedly to your spiritual development. This does not mean that you withdraw from your ordinary life. To the contrary. In the West our challenge is to walk on our chosen Path while remaining immersed in daily life.[1]

Dion Fortune (1891-1946), member of The Society of the Inner Light in England, was an outstanding teacher of esoteric thought. She wrote in *The Mystical Qabalah*, "The normal, healthy Westerner has no desire to escape from life, his urge is to conquer it and reduce it to order and harmony . . . the normal Western temperament demands 'life, more life'" (11). Yet a definite shift in your focus and values will occur when you decide to cooperate with your individualizing process.

You must make the journey essentially alone, that is, the strength to endure must be entirely your own. But the disciplines offered on a given Pathway can greatly facilitate the journey, and companionship and guidance are available. In fact, a powerful though invisible brother- and sisterhood binds together, across time and space, all who walk spiritual Pathways. Once you have made the decision to cooperate with your unfolding process, you will never need to feel alone again. Help and guidance will be available to you whenever you ask from the depth of your being.

You may wonder why you need to choose between Pathways, or what the value is of committing to a given Path. These words from Dion Fortune give her explanation:

> No student will ever make any progress in spiritual development who flits from system to system; first using

some New Thought affirmation, then some Yoga breathing exercises and meditation-postures, and following these by an attempt at the mystical methods of prayer. Each of these systems has its value, but that value can only be realized if the system is carried out in its entirety. They are the calisthenics of consciousness, and aim at gradually developing the powers of the mind. The value does not lie in the prescribed exercises as ends in themselves, but in the powers that will be developed if they are persevered with . . . we must choose our system and carry it out faithfully until we arrive, if not at its ultimate goal, at any rate at definite practical results and a permanent enhancement of consciousness. After this has been achieved we may, not without advantage, experiment with the methods that have been developed upon other Paths, and build up an eclectic technique and philosophy there from; but the student who sets out to be an eclectic before he has made himself an expert will never be anything more than a dabbler. (9)

All Pathways are valid and effective when pursued with devotion. All use the same methods, though with different intensity, frequency and focus. All require preparation and study if they are to be traversed without undue danger and delay along the way. All have the same end, even if labeled differently.

Because all Pathways to Union converge at the top of the mountain and become one, it is important to remember that the distinctions between the four we are outlining are not sharp. The Paths are not mutually exclusive. In fact, each shares characteristics with the others. Nevertheless, differentiations can be made, and it is most often true that an inclination toward one of the four predominates in a given individual.

## Polarities and Beyond

To walk on a spiritual Path is to cooperate consciously with the natural process of unfolding that occurs in our consciousness. I will attempt to summarize the important role that polarities play in our consciousness without going into this profound subject deeply. My intention is to help you appreciate how the Pathways differ in their way of working with polarities.

During the *infolding* phase of the creational process, consciousness was immersed in form. There was no knowing of self as separate from All that Is. All was One in unconsciousness.

When humanity came into form, an awakening began. Consciousness began to *unfold* from its profound sleep. We experienced this as a *loss* of Union. A gulf opened between "I" and "other." That made objective human consciousness possible. As we developed the ability to discriminate between self and others, polarization or dualism emerged as our principle way of viewing the world. We saw our world as made up of opposites such as hot and cold, pleasure and pain, good and evil.

It was the process of contrasting things that made it possible for us to make conscious choices between one thing and another. However, choice-making and the habit of contrasting and comparing increased our feeling that we were objects among other objects in a world of separate things. The pain of our feeling of separation from the world around us, including from the persons we loved most, became acute. In response, we began to long for Union, whether that longing was expressed as the search for a soul mate, as an intense sexual urge, as a deep desire to be recognized by another, or as a spiritual urge to know the Divine.

As we step onto a spiritual Pathway, we can use polarization as a way to move toward Union. Although that sounds like a contradiction, it is actually a way of saying that the human condition serves us as we unfold into more expanded states of consciousness. Here's how it works.

On the Path of Devotion, we choose the polarity of *self and other* as central. We focus on being of service to the other, including God, the Supreme Other. In the beginning we are still in the state of separation, thinking "I am self; but what matters most is the other." However, as we move toward Union we begin to discover that the more we serve others in Love, the more loving and loved we feel. Eventually it becomes clear that our loving service is benefiting both others *and* self. In the end we discover that we feel one with those we serve and with God, whom we serve *through* those others.

On the Path of Action, we choose the polarities of *actor and acted upon*, of *cause and effect*. Rather than experiencing ourselves as victims, that is, as those who are acted upon, we choose to identify ourselves as change agents, those who take action and affect the world around them. "To do" becomes our reason for being. As we move toward Union, we begin to understand that we *become* what we do, or that we *are* the effect because we are being the change we want to see happen. The polarities merge as doing and becoming become one.

On the Path of Contemplation we choose the polarity of *Truth and untruth*, or *Real and unreal*, as our focus. In the beginning we identify with untruth and believe we must *search for* what is True and Real. In time, we come to the awareness that we can only know the True and the Real by merging with it, by becoming one with it, by identifying with it. As the gap between self and the True and Real closes, the unreal and the untrue disappear from our consciousness.

On the Path of Self-Mastery we choose a dichotomy within self as our focus: *human and Divine, little self and higher self, body and soul, or body/soul and spirit.* As we struggle to master the functioning of the "lesser" self by appealing to the "higher" self, we come to know that we are both. When the inner dichotomy is healed, we experience our oneness with all others, for we recognize in them the One or Real Self that is also in us.

Full realization of our potential divinity will come when, in consciousness, we know that we are capable of doing all, of knowing all, and of being all. That is when we are able to consciously direct the activities, expressions, experiences, and articulations of Self. By whatever Path, we come to know that there is only One Self. The Truth lies in that Self. That Self acts only upon Itself.

It is this mystery that evokes gratitude, adoration, praise, worship, and recognition of the awesome magnitude of the experience that we call life. Knowing the Truth through direct experience, we are not afraid to experiment with the power of creation, to have experiences, and to apply what we have learned, for it is only through living that we come to Wisdom.

## Pursuing Freedom

In a very real sense, all who walk spiritual Pathways long to be free, but we talk about that freedom differently. One on the Path of Contemplation seeks to be free from illusion and falsehood in order to know the True and the Real. One on the Path of Self-Mastery wants to be free from bondage to unconscious functioning in order to master conscious self-expression in the world. One on the Path of Devotion longs to be free of emotional upheavals and addictions in order to Love unconditionally, universally, freely, gladly and in joy. And One on the Path of Action desires to be free of purposeless living and a sense of failure, a feeling of never being enough or doing enough. He wants to live fully, with passion and zest, doing his work with a light heart, in both gratitude and joy.

The liberation gained through this experience of Union is promised by all the great religions. In fact, the goal of the whole creating process, as perceived by seers in all times, is for the One Self to awaken consciously from within form and so to know itself as complete and whole, as free to be.

## Motivations for Stepping on a Path

Although all Paths lead to Union, those who choose to pursue their spiritual unfolding usually feel motivated by more specific expressions of the one urge.

One who walks the Path of Devotion might speak of a longing to experience Union with God. She would have a profound sense of an ineffable Presence in the world that is other than, or beyond, all that is manifest. This Presence would awaken in her a profound Love, which she would express through her acts of worship and prayer, as well as through loving service. She would understand her service to be *to God* in the guise of humanity, and her every act of service would be offered as an expression of her Love for and praise of the Almighty. In fact, she would almost rather remain in the *Presence* of God *as other* than to merge with God. She is one who is likely to be regarded by others as a saint or a radiant mystic, for her every act will be permeated with Love for the Divine.

One who walks the Path of Action might speak of a desire to be one with All. "All" would include not only the whole of humanity but also the world of nature and all other forms of life. He would seek this oneness through active service to the All in the world, and his greatest joy would be to lose himself in the work he does as service. He would not seek to transcend this world, but rather to transform it. To experience Union with All would liberate him to be an agent of transformation by so embodying the change he longs for that he becomes it. He is the quintessential humanitarian change agent.

The one who walks the Pathway of Contemplation has a compelling thirst for Truth. He wants to know what is Real in the world around him. He has a sense that "God" is merely an image in the mind of humanity, and that the world in which we live is like a meaningless play on an illusory stage. He has no faith that his own perception is any more valid than anyone else's, nor is he certain that there is a more fundamental, or real, Self to be discovered. But above all, he does not want to deceive himself with his own reasoning, and so he continues to search for what is True by learning to identify the Real. He is known as a philosopher or wise one.

On the Path of Self-Mastery one feels a longing to know the Real Self within and to master conscious manifestation of that Self in the world in order to consciously express the larger Will. Aware of a split within herself between the outer and inner selves, she seeks Union with the Real Self. Along the way she comes to know that there is only one Self, manifesting as the multitude that we call humanity. Therefore her quest for Union within merges with a quest for Union with the One and the All that others call God and humanity. Many will view her as a master teacher of the spiritual arts.

## Walking a Path

Both Devotion and Action are personal Pathways. That is, each focuses on expression through the personal self. The one walking the Path of Devotion focuses on the Solar Plexus Chakra, the center of personal feelings, both preferences and aversions. Since she longs to express her Love for God by being of service to human beings, the disciple on this Pathway needs to learn to lift those personal preferences into the Heart Center where they can be transformed into unconditional Love. However, she cannot escape the Solar Plexus. As she brings it into harmony with the Heart Chakra she finds that her greatest pleasure becomes giving herself in service to others. Her other preferences fall away and she expresses her Love for God in very personal and specific caring for other human beings.

She tends to function in the yin, or receptive, polarity. She prays to be guided and directed in her life, and thus is in a state of abundant expectancy, waiting for promptings of spirit. She embraces her life experience in whatever form it presents itself, receiving all people, situations, and even herself as beautiful exactly as they are. She sees herself as an open channel of God's Love flowing through her.

A disciple on this Pathway is focused on the concrete and specific. She will look for specific ways to be of service to specific individuals. And she will often seek out a specific Incarnation of the Divine to Love and adore. If she chooses such an Incarnation, she will ask for inspiration and guidance from this exemplar and will seek the blessing of his or her presence. She never dwells on herself, but rather keeps her eyes on her Beloved, the Other, whether in the image of an Incarnation of the Divine or in the myriad faces of humanity.

One walking the Path of Action also focuses on the Solar Plexus. His strong feelings about conditions and situations in the world around him motivate him to move into the Generative Chakra to bring some change into being. He is a personal agent for that change. He is immersed in life and involved with the people around him. Whatever he does awakens responses in others, and those responses are often directed at him, personally. The disciple on this Pathway seeks to stay true to his own deep-felt motivation as he moves into action, regardless of what others think of him or say to him or about him.

This disciple tends to function in the yang, or active, polarity of energy. Though he asks for guidance and inspiration, his focus is on moving into action. He is being the change he wants to see happen, and he does not wait for anyone else to be ready to join him or to approve of his actions. He, like the disciple walking the Devotional Path, is concrete and specific in his approach. He wants to know whom he can help and what he can bring into being.

He seeks an exemplar of his Path, not in order to have someone to worship or adore as an embodiment of the Divine, but rather to have someone to emulate. The disciple seeks to *become* what the exemplar has modeled. He pours his energy into being a change agent. He expresses his commitment in the way he lives his life and finds it helpful to have examples of others who have achieved the kind of integrity he seeks to embody. He is focused on self in that he requires of himself that he manifest his highest ideals.

Contemplation and Self-Mastery, on the other hand, are impersonal Pathways. The one walking the Path of Contemplation is focused in the Throat Chakra, using his mental processes to pursue the Truth, and in the Third Eye Center, seeking to see, to know, and to understand. His is a dispassionate quest for the True and Real, and he will persist even if he never sees any practical results and if he is never able to demonstrate in his own life any fruits of the search. In this sense, the approach of the contemplative is abstract. He is far more interested in the questions than in any practical application of the answers he might find. He is unwilling to commit himself to anything less than the Absolute.

One walking the Path of Contemplation tends to function in the yin, or magnetic, polarity of energy. He is constantly searching and asking, seeking to draw to himself the Truth he wants to know. Although his thought processes are active, he is not one to take action in the world or to urge others to action. His work is internal and largely hidden from the world around him. His attention is focused on other than himself, in the realm of the most abstract symbols and concepts possible to hold in mind.

He might seek out an exemplar of his Path to gain instruction in methods of contemplation and meditation. He might also enjoy studying with one who has come to his own knowing of the Truth. He might even hope to receive a direct transmission of perception or knowledge. In any case, his drawing would not be to the person so much as to the realization of Truth this person had achieved. His devotion, if offered, would not be to the individual but to the Truth.

The one walking the Path of Self-Mastery concentrates attention on her registry of energy in all chakras and on directing her self-expression on all levels. She is quite impersonal in her study of herself, taking the attitude of a scientific observer. She seeks to identify her patterns so that she can make conscious choices about the changes she wants to make in them. She practices directing herself in life situations as she might practice playing a musical instrument. She is not so much identified with her persona as she is interested in how the universal laws are at work in her. In all those ways she is more focused on self than on others, but her intent is to become a perfect instrument of the larger Will.

She tends to function in the yang, or active, polarity of energy since she is purposeful in directing her energy in all situations, even when she is sitting quietly in meditation. She takes responsibility for creating her own reality consciously and chooses consciously how to receive from others as well as how to express herself to them.

One on this Pathway seeks teachers who can help her to learn the laws and principles that will lead to self-understanding. She also wants to learn many techniques to help her to gain Self-Mastery. She does not *follow* her teachers in a personal way. Rather, she takes the Wisdom she learns from them and applies it in her laboratory of self, keeping what works for her and letting the rest fall away. The teachers serve as examples for her only to the extent that they have mastered their own self-expression in the world.

## What Is a Disciple?

In the great spiritual traditions, you are considered a Seeker until you approach the mountain to make your solo climb. At that time you become a disciple. A disciple is one who, through the intuition, finds the Path that fits his or her own nature and makes a conscious choice to follow disciplines representative of that Path.

Prior to setting out on your solitary journey as a disciple, you will have prepared yourself by getting into "shape." That is, you will have gained physical, emotional and mental health, and you will have established consistency between your inner and outer lives, between what you know about yourself and what you express as self in the world. You will have done your physical and psychological work and have developed what is usually termed a strong and integrated nature, or ego.

As you walk your chosen Way, you may discover new levels of psychological and/or physical work that need to be done, because consciousness expands spherically. As you open to higher frequencies of energy, you are likely to discover more in the personal and group psyche to bring into your conscious awareness. You may find that you need to step aside, as though going to a "clinic," to attend to psychological or physical needs before continuing on your Way. That kind of integrative work is an essential part of your journey.

When you begin your individualizing journey, you consciously accept responsibility for your own life, knowing that you can no longer blame your personal history, other persons in your acquaintance, or your life circumstances when you stumble. Nor can you give anyone else the credit for the progress you make. This does not mean that you will be all alone throughout your trek, but it does mean that you alone can make the journey, and you alone will take the credit or blame for what happens to you along the way. Thus the disciple is a mature adult who is financially and emotionally independent, or at least has the capacity to become that should the journey so require. That is, the disciple is capable of making choices that do not conform to the patterns and preferences of his loved ones, and to act on those choices. He is not bound up in co-dependent relationships.

Similarly, when you step on a spiritual Path, you leave behind the habit of looking for intervention from outside to "save" you because of some feeling of unworthiness. Instead, you take responsibility for developing the strengths you need, which are inherent within you, and for bringing your expression into balance so that your perfect pattern can become manifest. You make an inner commitment to a disciplined life of cooperation with the natural order process. Your primary work is to facilitate the unfolding of the pattern imprinted in your energy field and held in the core of Self, like a soul-seed. You decide in the depths of your inner being that becoming all that you have the potential to become is more important to you than anything else.

You choose your Path according to your own focus in consciousness, your personal style, and the guidance of your inner being. Because the commitment is an internal one, it does not require association with an outer group, or even involvement in outer study or with a spiritual teacher. In the inner silence of your own being, you make a commitment to bring your knowing into expression through thought, word and deed. All outer action from that time onward is measured and evaluated by you against the standard of your own commitment.

You may choose to participate in some group, to engage in a particular course of study, or to give yourself over to the direction and guidance of a teacher, guru, world teacher, Master, or Divine Incarnation. You welcome the reflection of the outer as you walk your inner Path. Nevertheless, your own inner commitment remains the overseeing authority and measure of the value of your group participation, of the teachings, and of the role an outer guide serves in your unfolding process.

From the time you step on a spiritual Path, you will have no other authority than the inner Self with whom and as whom you set your course. Whatever you learn from another, or whatever guidance you accept from another, you incorporate into your life and consciousness because it is in harmony with your inner authority. When you participate in groups and join them in activities, it is because doing so furthers your own chosen purposes and objectives.

As a disciple, you will find companions on the Way, and you will discover that the support and encouragement they offer is quite different from what you have experienced as friendship and "belonging" until now. Companions on spiritual Pathways support you in your purpose as you seek Union with the Divine, and encourage you in your chosen disciplines. They often don't, however, share common interests with you on the personality level, nor engage in personally nourishing activities with you. You will learn to accept their spiritual nourishment while meeting your personal needs with other friends.

As a disciple, you exercise your will in order to continue your climb when the ascent is difficult or you have suffered a setback. You need your will to sustain the disciplines you have chosen, for no one can hold you to your commitment through punishment or reminder. You need to have the ability to sustain your purpose under all circumstances and to use your disciplines to strengthen your will.

As a disciple, you may find a teacher who will give you guidance and direction and who will be able to pass on the tradition of accumulated Wisdom gathered by those who have gone before you. However, your teacher will not be responsible for infusing you with inspiration, for reassuring you when you are in trouble, for rescuing you from danger, or for supporting you when you grow weak. The teacher can offer you much from his or her own experience on the Path, but you must do your own walking on your own power or you will not accomplish the individualizing process that the Path represents.

As a disciple, you want only one thing: to fulfill

your self-selected purpose. How you formulate that purpose will depend on the Pathway you have chosen. But your focus needs to be singular if you are to continue to live out that purpose even when you feel discouraged or frustrated because things don't appear to be going well in your life. You need to be able to accept both pain and pleasure as inherent to the life process.

You control your mind so that it serves you and your purpose, rather than undermining you with doubts and criticisms. You use your trained and honed mind to discriminate the Real from the unreal, so that your journey will be grounded in the substance of Self and integrated in your daily life. It is too easy for spirituality to become a flight into glamour or idealism or grandiose images of the Divine. In those cases, visions become fantasies rather than realities.

Your profound desire to be free from all that binds you and divides you fuels a great power of endurance. Spiritual development takes a long time and can be difficult, and once you set out, it is almost impossible to turn back. This is because once you have acknowledged the inner urge, you will find it relentless in the pressure it exerts from within.

For all these reasons, Seekers study and prepare before setting out on a spiritual Path.


## Spiritual Disciplines

No matter what Path one walks toward Union, time alone for quiet reflection is central. All treaders on Pathways seek to still the objective mind, and eventually to clear it of its automatic thinking. All seek to quiet the emotions, and eventually to free them of unconscious reactions that create turbulence within. All seek to relax the body, and eventually to calm it so that it does not demand attention. And for all, these objectives make it possible to focus awareness and to direct energy according to an overall purpose.

The disciple on the Devotional Path holds purposes such as to know God, to Love and praise God, and to be of service to God. Working with feelings, the disciple on this Pathway spends her quiet time in activities such as prayer, chanting, singing, saying mantras, and participating in rituals and ceremonies. She seeks to awaken feelings of praise, thanksgiving, joy, devotion, and unconditional Love. She looks forward to just one experience of the full Presence of God, which she knows will last for a lifetime. If she has such an experience, she will point to it for the rest of her life.

The disciple on the Action Path holds purposes such as to know All, to be one with All, to serve humanity, and to make a difference in the world. Working with creative vital energy, the disciple on this Pathway spends his quiet time in activities such as Hatha Yoga, walking meditation, playing or listening to music, working on a creative project (building, sculpting, painting, etc.), and active meditation (holding a focus while doing a chosen daily task). He seeks to awaken passion for intentional action. He is not so much focused on having an experience of Union as he is on what he will do as a *result* of such an experience.

The disciple on the Contemplative Path holds purposes such as to know Truth and to identify what is Real. Working with the mind, the disciple on this Pathway spends his quiet time in activities such as concentrated study and thought, contemplation of questions, repeating mantras, and deep meditation.

He seeks to awaken understanding and direct perception, and such an experience is all that matters to him.

The disciple on the Self-Mastery Path holds purposes such as to know the Real Self, to be one with Self, and to consciously direct experience and self-expression. Working with the will, the disciple on this Pathway spends her quiet time in activities such as Hatha Yoga, chanting, saying mantras, concentrated study, breath work, contemplation on the chakras, directing energy, and deep meditation. She seeks to arouse the higher Will through persistence, steadiness, and determination. If she catches a glimpse of the Real Self, she wants to learn how to sustain that awareness in every living moment.

## Spiritual Teachers

Finding a spiritual teacher once you have chosen your Pathway is a matter of following your heart and your inner guidance. You will be guided to a contact, and then to another, until you find someone with whom you will have an awakening relationship. The relationship with the teacher will help to rouse you from the sleep of unconsciousness into more of your potential. If you were a young shoot pushing through the ground of your Being, a spiritual teacher would be like the sun, which warms and encourages the growth already taking place.

My teacher, Vitvan, offered a description of the urge that moves in us once we step on a Path. This description comes out of the ancient tradition of Wisdom teachings:

It has been said that the Limitless Light can be defined in a single word, "pressure." The Absolute – or God, if you wish – is pressure. Its out-flowing force is irresistible. Nothing can stay its hand or stem its course. When awareness begins to awaken in man it is the advent of that pressure within his individualized consciousness. (Satriano 35)

When you begin to notice that pressure from within, you will feel you have no choice but to go where you are moved to go and do what you are moved to do. That inner pressure will direct you to a spiritual teacher.

A spiritual teacher is more than just an instructor who can teach you techniques or concepts. He or she is a Light-bearer. This is a function analogous to one candle igniting another or the sun coming in through the window in the morning, stirring us from our sleep. A spiritual teacher is a disciple who is climbing the mountain along a particular Pathway and is doing the very process of unfolding that he or she describes. Associating with such a person will help to kindle the fire of devotion within you. You will benefit from the accumulated Wisdom this one is able to impart to you according to his or her own understanding.

As the student you must be discriminating, however, for it is not the spiritual teacher's role or function to offer a personal model for the living of your life. The teacher will show you the way to *walk,* not the way to *live.* If you as a student imitate your teacher's character, work or life-style, you may not only hamper progress on your chosen spiritual Path, but you may even go astray. You must listen to your inner guidance for the living of your daily life, for you have a destiny that is yours alone. The spiritual disciplines your teacher will offer will help you find the way to your source of inner knowing.

Martin Buber, the great Jewish philosopher, illustrates this point with a story:

> . . . When the disciples of a deceased zaddik [wise man] came to the "Seer" of Lublin and expressed surprise at the fact that his customs were different from those of their late master, the "Seer" exclaimed: "What sort of God would that be who has only one way in which he can be served!" But by the fact that each man, starting from his particular place and in a manner determined by his particular nature, is able to reach God, God can be reached by mankind as such, through its multiple advance by all those different ways. (18)

We could use the analogy of a lamp along a walkway. It sheds light that helps you to see as you walk there. If you look at the lamp itself, you cannot see the path. You must look at the path in the light being shed by the lamp and keep walking if you are to make progress. In a similar way, to focus on your spiritual teacher is at best only a diversion.

A teacher is someone who sheds Light on your chosen Way. The Light he or she sheds will be dim or relatively brighter according to the degree of his/her own expansion of consciousness, and the Light will be "colored" according to the degree the teacher has yet to purify his or her own psyche.

A teacher is more a function than a person. That is to say, your teacher(s) will be the one(s) you feel you can learn from. With the one(s) you recognize as teacher(s) you will have a resonance in consciousness, which means that the teacher will quicken, by his/her presence, your inner urge to growth, mirror your inner knowing, and illumine your Way because he/she is walking "in your vicinity."

In the Eastern traditions there is a saying, "When the student is ready the teacher will appear." This means that you as student have sufficiently prepared yourself to recognize the teacher, and that you have brought yourself into the teacher's proximity.

This concept is important to grasp. It removes the implication that the teacher appears out of nowhere, and it discourages the tendency to aggrandize the teacher. In the great spiritual traditions, it is always understood that all spiritual boons are earned. That is, what comes to you is a result of your own process of unfolding, your own developmental labor.

Consider how children become adults. They do not remain children until one magic day when someone appears in their lives and grants them adulthood. No. They achieve adulthood through the labor of growing up. That developmental process is hard work. Those of us who have accomplished it know that there were many obstacles to overcome. There was much pain. There were also the rewards of fun and pleasure and a sense of accomplishment. But no one could do the growing up for us. We all had to do it for ourselves. And if we didn't accomplish certain maturational tasks during our childhood or teen years, they remained to be executed later, in those years called adulthood. As a result, many of us do not become adults until our middle years, and some of us never fully manage it. We remain children, to one degree or another, till the end of our lives.

It is the same in the spiritual realm. The individualizing process cannot begin until the body and personality are mature. Therefore, it is a developmental work for adults only. Once that phase of the unfolding process begins, it is the individual who is doing it in the laboratory of Self. Your teacher(s) will appear because you are ready to study. That is, you will have prepared yourself sufficiently to be able to receive what a teacher has to offer. It is like saying, "After traveling for three hours, a fork in the road appeared." It did not appear magically. You had gone far enough to find it.

You may find a teacher you can study with in person. It is equally possible to find your teacher through books or on inner planes. But until such a time, you will be able to begin your ascent following general guidelines such as are given in this book and others, and following your own inner direction. As you walk, however, you will meet others who speak of their teachers and you will want to understand that relationship.

Most who walk the Path of Devotion need or want a teacher or a Divine Incarnation to whom they can surrender their total devotion. One on the Karma Pathway looks for a teacher by whose side he can walk and whose example he can follow. One walking the Path of Contemplation longs for a teacher with whom he can meditate. And one on the Self-Mastery Pathway looks for a teacher who can act as coach, inculcating techniques and skills and encouraging mastery of them.

**World Teachers** communicate Truth cross-culturally and offer guidance that can be trusted regardless of your personally chosen religion or Pathway. Tenzin Gyatso, the fourteenth Dalai Lama of Tibet, is one who is recognized as a World Teacher in our time.

People of all religious traditions respect him, and his counsel and advice are quite universally received as sound.

**Gurus** (a term that comes out of Eastern traditions) are teachers who embody a given Pathway. They illumine the Path by leading the way. Disciples can travel with them, being strengthened and encouraged by their presence and example. Their Light is stronger, brighter and clearer because of their own development, and in their presence disciples experience states of consciousness that are beyond them, but are illumined for them by the guru.

In the Eastern tradition, gurus have within their own Being the power to light the spark of Divine awareness within another. Believing in that function, parents entrust their children to the care and upbringing of a guru, who educates their souls to the knowing of their true nature and lights the fire of all-consuming desire to know the Divine.

Generally speaking, gurus and disciples enter into a special relationship characterized by a commitment to one another. Gurus agree to take on responsibility for their disciples' development, and thus to share in their karma. Disciples, in turn, agree to be unequivocally faithful to their gurus, revealing the truth of their states of awareness and trusting without questioning the guidance and admonition of their gurus.

Needless to say, you would need to know yourself very well before entering into such a relationship, for the guru becomes an outer representation of your own higher nature. To trust the guru is to trust yourself. To recognize the guru is to see in the outer what you have come to know within.

In the East, the function of the guru is taken very seriously and cannot be transferred into our Western culture without highly developed discrimination. It would be well to study with other spiritual teachers until you have purified your own psyche and developed your own spiritual faculties. Then you would be able to recognize someone as a true guru before entering into such a commitment.

**A Master** is one who has climbed the spiritual mountain and come to know Union with the Divine and within Self. Such a one, if living in the world, may be making a contribution through a given art form, profession or trade, and thus be widely recognized as a "genius," outstanding personality, or great leader. She may be leading an obscure and seemingly ordinary life, or she may be spearheading a spiritual renewal as a reformer or teacher. We might think of Leonardo da Vinci and Shakespeare as examples of Masters, just to grasp the idea. Or, such a one may no longer be embodied in human form. These Beings often have jobs to do in the Whole *other than teaching*, and may not have much patience with those who are in the early stages of their spiritual development.

**A Divine Incarnation** is one who perfectly embodies all Paths and whose Light is so bright and so clear that to look into him or her is to see the Light of Divinity shining through. Such a one is the embodiment of the highest state of development to which a human can aspire. These are the Teachers of all spiritual teachers. They can transmit spirituality with a touch, even with a mere glance. Swami Vivekananda says, "We cannot see God except through them. We cannot help worshipping them; indeed they are the only ones whom we are bound to worship" (37). Jesus is reported to have said about himself: "Anyone who has seen me has seen the Father" (John 14:9b).

In the course of human history there have been relatively few Divine Incarnations. Even those who are widely, if not unanimously, honored as highly developed or even enlightened teachers and/or prophets are not universally acknowledged as Divine Incarnations. Perhaps the three most generally accepted as Incarnations are Krishna, Gautama Buddha, and Jesus. Others recognized by large numbers of persons are: Hermes, Zoroaster (Zarathustra), Ramakrishna and (alive in our present age) Sathya Sai Baba. In addition, there are many who, if not recognized as Incarnations, are at least revered as Prophets of God. Among them are Abraham, Moses, Mohammed, the Bab, the Baal Shem Tov, Amitabha and Laotzu.

Most of us have access to those who are called Divine Incarnations primarily through the teachings recorded by their disciples in holy books, or scriptures. Often the teachings of gurus are also available through their own writings and/or their designated representatives: disciples who teach the guru's way. Less developed teachers are more widely accessible through their own writings, classes and talks. They usually stand in a lineage that includes a master teacher, a guru and/or Divine Incarnation.

There are three characteristics especially worthy of consideration in evaluating teachers.

First, do the teachers know the spirit of all the great scriptures and show respect for the highest in all traditions of spiritual teaching? This you will recognize, not only by what they are able to teach you, but also by their willingness to acknowledge their own limitations and mistakes, and to express gratitude for and pay tribute to the contributions of others to their own growth. Moreover, they will pay less attention to the details of a given text than to what the text reveals, and will acknowledge the One Truth expressed in and through the various religious and spiritual traditions.

The inner spirit of all scriptures is universal and all embracing. Teachers, if they know that Truth, will not be any less comprehensive in their own presentations of the Wisdom.

Second, do the teachers do their work as an expression of unconditional Love, rather than to accumulate wealth, recognition, fame, power and/or influence? In our Western culture it is natural for teachers to charge for their classes for two reasons. Students generally do not value what is offered for free, since monetary value is our primary way of assessing things. And our culture places a high value on earning your own way rather than depending on the beneficence of others. Nevertheless, if spiritual teachers have unmet ego needs for wealth, fame, or power, these may get in the way of their clear representation of the Wisdom.

Third, do the teachers honor the individuality of their students? All who have stepped onto spiritual Paths recognize that each one must make this journey essentially alone. The process to be undergone is an individualizing process. You must bring forth conscious knowing from within your own field of awareness. For that reason, genuine teachers of the Wisdom will honor and respect the individuality of each disciple. They will not require conformity to a group at the expense of individual integrity, nor will they demand obedience when the disciple's inner direction is in conflict.

If teachers meet these tests of their sincerity and integrity, then you can more confidently entrust yourself to their instruction, be humble in their presence, submit to the disciplines they suggest, and hold them in high regard.

Should the time come when a given teacher illumines only what you already know and have integrated in your daily living, it will be time to move on to a brighter Light, or one farther along your Pathway. Offer gratitude for what you have received, but do not cling to the form through which you received it.

---

1. See P.D. Ouspensky, *The Fourth Way,* New York: Vintage Books, 1971.

**Works Cited**
The New English Bible.
Buber, Martin. *The Way of Man: According to the Teachings of Hasidism.* Chicago: A Cloister Press Book, 1951.
Fortune, Dion. *The Mystical Qabalah.* York Beach, ME: Samuel Weiser, Inc., 2000.
Richard Satriano, *Vitvan: An American Master.* Baker, NV: School of the Natural Order, 1977.
Vivekananda, Swami. *Bhakti-Yoga: The Yoga of Love and Devotion.* Calcutta, India: Advaita Ashrama, 1978.

# RELIGIONS
# AND PATHWAYS

*The exoteric, state-organized section of
the Christian Church persecuted and
stamped out the esoteric section, destroy-
ing every trace of its literature upon
which it could lay hands in striving to
eradicate the very memory of a gnosis
from human history.*

*— Dion Fortune*

Western culture suffered a particular kind of dep-
rivation beginning in the third century after the time
of Jesus when the Roman Emperor Constantine made
Christianity the religion of the Empire. Constantine
wanted a religion that would unify his diverse empire,
and he chose Christianity primarily because his
mother was a convert and believer. In order to accomplish unification, he changed the name of Pagan holi-
days and made them Christian celebrations instead,
and he systematically destroyed all expressions of
competing religions and all aspects of Christianity that
could not be controlled by his secular authority.

The Christian Gnosis had passed along keys to
the Wisdom Teachings during the first two centuries
after Jesus lived. These keys were the secrets Jesus

taught to his disciples and which were at the heart of the parables he gave to the masses.[1] However, since the Gnosis had been given only to the few who were willing to undergo a rigorous training under the guidance and direction of masters who embodied the Wisdom, Constantine recognized that he could not bring the Gnosis under his rule. Consequently, he ordered all references to it to be stricken from the New Testament and all expressions of it to be eradicated from his empire. The result was that Christianity was deprived of the life-giving inner tradition upon which it was originally founded.[2]

Not only were Christians denied direct access to the spiritual meaning of their tradition, but they were also taught to distrust all expressions of the Wisdom and to view them as the work of the devil. That distrust continues to permeate Western culture to this day, even though the Church has lost much of its power and authority in today's world.

One way to think about the relationship of religions to Pathways is to view religions as the outer body of spirituality in a culture; traditions, celebrations, and beliefs can be seen as the soul or psyche of spirituality; and Pathways can be understood to represent the spirit itself. If the spirit dies or is suppressed, the heart goes out of the psyche; traditions, celebrations, and beliefs become empty shells that convey little if any meaning. The body may live on for a long time, but its vitality gradually wanes and it commands little inner authority.

Religions are the outer, exoteric expression of inner, esoteric spirituality. Spirituality is termed esoteric because it is not accessible to the five senses and therefore is only understood by those who have developed what Jesus called "the eyes to see," namely the capacity to register and experience subtle energies beyond what we usually call the physical or material world.

All world religions came into existence because a great teacher or prophet had experienced those inner, subtle realms. The vitality of his life and teachings was an expression of the depth of his inner life, and disciples followed who longed to experience and know in their own lives what the teacher or prophet exemplified. Consequently, each of the world religions bears a strong resemblance, in its teachings, rituals, traditions and practices (in its "psyche"), to the spiritual Pathway walked by the putative founder or to the predilections of the early disciples of that founder. I say "putative" founder because most religions were in fact organized by disciples of the original prophet or teacher rather than by the man himself.

Each world religion focuses on the entrance to one of the Four Pathways to Union. However, smaller groups within the main religions often choose to emphasize different Pathways because of their own inclinations and preferences.

## RELIGIONS and The Devotional Pathway

Disciples of Jesus of Nazareth developed the religion we know today as Christianity. The disciples believed Jesus, who revealed to them that God is Love, to be an Incarnation of God. The term "Christ" came out of the esoteric perception that Jesus had been anointed by the inner Holy Spirit. The term "Christ" was based on the Greek word *christos*, meaning anointed. Thus, Jesus, the Christed or anointed one, became known as Jesus Christ and has been the central focus of Christian worship for nearly two thousand years.

Hinduism, also sometimes called the Vedic religion after the Holy Scriptures on which it is based, the Vedas, developed in a similar fashion several millennia before the time of Jesus. Krishna is remembered as the Divine Incarnation who exemplified the spirit of Love and devotion that permeates Hinduism. Stories of his life inspire Hindus to this day, although he is not perceived to be the *only* Incarnation of God as Jesus is in Christianity. In fact, Hindus believe there have been thousands of Incarnations of the Divine and they feel no conflict over which image of the Divine to choose as the focus of their daily devotional practices.

In both religions, devotional practices such as prayer, worship, hymn singing or chanting, and rituals reflect the spiritual Pathway of the individual who is totally devoted to knowing God in a Love-Union.

Although the other world religions are not primarily devotional in nature, within each of them a representation of the Devotional Path has developed in response to the need of those within their groups who are devotional by temperament.

Mahayana Buddhism has become the largest branch of a religion that began with a focus on the Pathway of Contemplation. Mahayana Buddhism provides those who are devotional by nature an outlet for their adoration of Gautama and other Incarnations of buddhic consciousness. Although Gautama is often referred to simply as "The Buddha," that appellation is similar to calling Jesus "The Christ." A "Buddha" is one whose consciousness has been enlightened by the buddhic light of Truth.

Buddhist churches of the Mahayana tradition in the West have taken on an outer form that is not very different from many branches of Christianity. Many have congregational worship, with hymn singing, scripture reading, and preaching. Styles of worship in Eastern cultures are more individualized, but nevertheless in the Mahayana branch of Buddhism devotion has taken the place of contemplation and meditation as the primary expression of religious commitment.

Islam traditionally emphasizes the path of law (*sharia*), and thus, along with Judaism, can be considered a reflection of the Pathway of Action. However, in the ninth century a major popular religious movement developed within Islam to provide an interior mystical Way (*tariqa*). That movement is called Sufism. This spiritual discipline provided a method by which the individual Muslim could not only follow but also *know* God. Renunciation and purification (disciplining the mind and body) were practiced in order to directly experience the Ultimate Reality. Their name derived from their practice of wearing simple, coarse woolen (*suf*) garments.

Sufism developed as a parallel, popular movement within Islam and helped Islam to become the second largest world religion. The Sufis became the great missionaries and popular preachers of Islam in Asia and Africa, and Sufi Brotherhoods were formed to provide communal centers for devotees. By the seventeenth century, however, Sufism had fallen into the excesses to which the Devotional Pathway can easily lead, and it fell into disrepute.

The inner core of the tradition was nevertheless passed on through the lineage of Sufi masters, largely in secrecy. In our time there is a revival of interest in

Sufism by Muslims and others seeking a viable Devotional Pathway for their own inner development.[3]

In Judaism, the Pathway of Devotion is found in the Hassidic movement. Hassidism sought to popularize the esoteric teachings of Judaism, the Qabalah, and taught that man could become one with God. Individuals ready to do God's will were in a perpetual search for opportunities to be of service. They were encouraged to carry every *mitzvah* (good deed) beyond the limits described in the Torah, inventing new instruments of service to the Divine.

The mass movement of Hassidism which emerged in the southern provinces of 18th century Poland taught that life is for the sake of the Love of God, and Love is best cultivated in joy, and in the discovery of new, individualistic ways of serving Him. Love is an anticipation *in feeling* of Union with the Beloved. It can become so intense and deep as to make every action a sacrament of faith.

These devotees emerged from a religious tradition based on the Pathway of Action, which does not focus on an embodied representative of the Divine. Nevertheless, Hassidism formed a new ideal of the religious leader, the *Zaddik.* Gershom Scholem, in his book *Major Trends in Jewish Mysticism,* observes that this focus introduced something entirely new. "*Personality* takes the place of *doctrine* (344)" and the living saint, the *Zaddik* became a dwelling place for the *Shechinah* (the Radiance). This made the Hassidic movement an appropriate vehicle for the Path of Devotion as well as the Path of Action.

Hassidism introduced the goal of mystical ecstasy into Jewish worship, trained its devotees to seek the inwardness of piety, aroused the feelings of joy and enthusiasm in prayer and, in general, translated the legalistic chores of Judaism into living expressions of a felt religious reality. Yet, it directed its impetus into the community, bringing into being the Hassidic society, which consisted of a loosely organized band of families, scattered in various cities, who traveled to and followed the guidance of their spiritual master, called a *Rebbe* or a *Zaddik*. (Scholem, 342)

The examples of persons who have experienced Union with the Divine by walking the Devotional Pathway are numerous over the course of history. However, even in Christianity and Hinduism, which are primarily devotional in their orientation, it is the rare person who is *totally* devoted to praise, adoration, Love and devotion, and to living a life of service as an expression of that spirit. Persons who are that devout often choose a monastic order for the expression of their vocation. Therefore, they are set apart from the ordinary practitioners of the religion.

First of all, the religions themselves are authoritarian in their structure. Priests, ministers, rabbis, or immans have an important place in these great religions. Their cultic roles tend to supersede the importance of the rituals as expressions of *personal* devotion. The fervor of those totally committed to walking the Devotional Pathway is focused on *God*. Clergy may feel their cultic roles are not sufficiently honored by such devotion.

Moreover, to curb the emotionalism of this Pathway, religions have developed creeds and belief-systems to which followers are expected to adhere. The priests or other leaders become the authorities who determine whether an individual's beliefs are correct.

Persons who experience the firey transformation of the Heart-Union with God no longer accept outer voices of authority. They do not hesitate to call into question church teachings that violate the spirit of Love. Encouraging such individuals to join monastic orders helps to confine their influence on the laity to manageable boundaries, although they often remain troublesome to their superiors. It is often not until after their deaths that they are offered as examples to the laity of true faith in the religion.

One fine example of this latter process is Gautama Buddha, who started a movement of reform within Hinduism that was so full of Truth that it eventually spread around the world. In India, however, Buddhism almost disappeared after Gautama's death because the Hindu priests declared Gautama to have been an Incarnation of the Divine. He therefore became an appropriate object of worship *within Hinduism* as another manifestation of the Divine. Shrines were provided in all major Hindu temples so that devotees could worship the Buddha within Hinduism. The essence of the Buddha's teachings, meanwhile, which would have constituted a reform of Hinduism, almost completely fell away. Only in other cultures, such as Nepal, Sri Lanka, Burma, Thailand, Japan, China and Tibet, did the teachings flower and bear fruit.

## RELIGIONS and the Path of Action

The two great world religions that reflect the Path of Action are Judaism and Islam. Judaism is based on the Law introduced by the prophet Moses. Prophets are believed to reveal Divine Will. Moses brought Ten

Commandments that were to serve as the foundation of a new society based on law. The Israelites agreed to obey the commandments as a sign of their covenant with God. They would live in obedience to Divine Law and God, in response, would bless them.

Islam arose as a reform of Judaism. The prophet Mohammed proclaimed that the Jews had fallen away from the Covenant with God. He taught his followers to purify their religious practice by offering prayers five times a day, by giving alms to the poor, by journeying to Mecca, and by fasting once a year. These practices were to enable the followers of Islam to live a better life, more faithful to God's law.

Although Christianity has Devotion as its primary Pathway, it honors and respects its roots in Judaism through the large emphasis in Christianity on what is called social action. This is a reflection of the Pathway of Action and it is retained as the secondary focus of most Christian churches. In Catholicism, the emphasis has been on Christian charity, namely acts of kindness done for the poor. Charity is more properly an expression of the Path of Devotion, because it does not address the societal roots of poverty, for example.

In Protestant churches the Path of Action has received greater emphasis. Protestants have not only focused on the establishment of hospitals and educational institutions around the world, as have Catholics, but they have encouraged their members to take stands on political issues and to participate in community action projects that are designed to bring about concrete change in the way society functions. In the 1980's, the Roman Catholic Church in Latin American countries adopted an even more radical movement called liberation theology. It supported active intervention to change the political structures that oppress the poor.

In Hinduism, the principle expression of the Path of Action is in the belief people hold in what is called Karma. The Vedas teach that in each successive lifetime our circumstances are determined by our actions in the previous lifetime. Therefore, nearly all Hindus believe that it is essential to do good works in the world in order to improve their lot in their next life. The result is that Hindus hold to strong moral codes and find joy in doing small acts of kindness. Within the philosophy of Yoga, which is a branch of Hinduism, there is a complete presentation of the Path of Action in what is called Karma Yoga.

Although Buddhism does not have a formal expression of the Path of Action, the eight-fold Path, taught by Gautama, includes right conduct, which includes doing no harm to others and being compassionate and kind to all creatures that have life. It also includes right livelihood, which means earning one's living from a work that does not harm others. Thus there is broad philosophical support for those who are inclined to the Path of Action.

However, neither Buddhism nor Hinduism evokes quite the same direct societal intervention that Judaism, Islam, and even some sects of Christianity emphasize. This is because for Buddhists and Hindus right action is housed within a larger world view that places more emphasis on what will follow this life than it does on this lifetime itself.

# RELIGIONS
## and the Path of Contemplation

The world religion that reflects the Path of Contemplation is Buddhism. The religion formed around Siddartha Gautama, who came into buddhic consciousness by applying his reason to the problem of suffering in the world. He sought to understand why there was suffering, and through his contemplation, which deepened into meditation, he broke through to a direct perception of the Truth of the human dilemma. Gautama chose to turn from his immersion in buddhic bliss back to objective consciousness where he could teach others how to gain freedom from their suffering.

Gautama did not establish a new religion. Rather, he sought to reform the Vedic religion into which he was born as it was practiced in his day, just as Jesus sought to reform Judaism nearly 500 years later. Gautama, like all great religious teachers of all times and cultures, knew that true spirituality did not lie in creed or cult, but rather in the direct experience of each individual. This primary truth, that one must realize God in one's own soul (Prabhavananda 173), is central for all Pathways and for the great exemplars of all religions, though it is not always taught by religions.

However, because Gautama's enlightenment was complete, his teachings, like the teachings of Jesus, comprehend all Pathways. Consequently it did not take long for Buddhism to divide into two major branches: Theravada and Mahayana. Theravada Buddhism, prevalent in Sri Lanka, Burma and Thailand, continues to have the Path of Contemplation as its primary emphasis. Mahayana Buddhism, practiced in China, Japan, and in the West, shifts over to a Devotional Pathway, as was described above. Tibetan Buddhism and the Buddhism practiced in Mongolia incorporate elements of the Pathways of Self-Mastery and Action as well Devotion and Contemplation.

In our times, Tibetan Buddhism is becoming more widely known in the West because so many practitioners are in exile. However, it is the Tibetans' focus on compassion, and therefore the Path of Action, that has captured the world's imagination, especially as expressed and represented by the Dalai Lama.

Zen Buddhism, however, which comes to the West from Japan, is an expression of the Path of Contemplation that is finding wide acceptance in the West. Zen Buddhism took the Chinese philosophy of the Tao, which lends itself more properly to the Path of Action, and wedded it to Buddhism, which reflected the Path of Contemplation. The result was something very appealing to those Westerners who are by nature inclined to inner reflection but who share the West's value on staying active in the world. In particular, the practice of Vipassana Meditation, often referred to as Mindfulness, has gained popularity in the West.

In Judaism, which primarily reflects the Path of Action, there have been philosophers, lovers of wisdom, from very early times. However, perhaps the most powerful philosophical movement within Judaism arose in the middle ages, receiving its classic formulation in the philosophy of Moses Maimonides (1135 -1204). To Maimonides the universe was bigger than the Torah and life was bigger than the law. Thus he believed Jews should study the Talmud in order to learn the laws of Judaism that were needed for guidance in daily living. But then he taught that the Jew should turn his mind to the study and contemplation of the basic truths of life. According to this view, as Gershom Scholem expresses it, "the rational faculty latent in the mind is actualized in the process of cognition, and this realization of the intellect is the sole guide to immortality (240)". Maimonides' *Guide to the Perplexed* exercised a great influence on Jewish history even though Maimonides was highly criticized by exponents of rabbinic tradition.[4]

In Christianity, which centers on the Path of Devotion, those inclined to the Path of Contemplation have been hard pressed to find a context in which to pursue their mental proclivities. At the time of Jesus and Paul, Gnostics (which means literally "those who know") walked that Way, but in the third century a schism formed between the main stream of Christianity, by then centered in Rome, and the Gnostics, who were concentrated in Greece. Gnosticism was declared a heresy by Rome, and since that time people who raise questions about matters of doctrine and belief are viewed with suspicion and are frequently ostracized or banned. In recent years several Roman Catholic theologians have been defrocked or removed from their teaching posts because they pursued reason beyond what the Church defines as the boundaries of belief.

Most Christian Schools of Theology do not encourage the quest for Union with the Divine, let alone teach one to use reason to achieve that Union. In the Roman Catholic Church, however, the Jesuit Order (the Society of Jesus) was formed and given an imprimatur by the Pope specifically for persons who wished to devote themselves to study and pursuits of the intellect as their way of expressing devotion to God. Thus some small provision was made within the Christian religion for persons walking the Pathway of Contemplation.

Hinduism, also primarily a devotionally oriented religion, offers six branches of philosophy within orthodoxy. That is, all six accept the authority of the Vedas (the four sacred books of Hinduism) in questions pertaining to the nature of the universe. Any of these systems of thought would serve a Hindu who sought to walk the Pathway of Contemplation. The two branches of Vedic philosophy best known in the West are Vedanta and Yoga. All six schools focus on *moksa* (enlightenment) as the highest attainment and all are concerned with the nature of the true Self, the immediate experience of which makes one free.

Yoga is concerned with the practical side of philosophical and religious life and in its essence can be said to be an expression of the Path of Self-Mastery, but it offers the Jnana-Yoga Path for those inclined to reason. Vedanta, on the other hand, is accepted as the belief system to which modern Hindus (who pursue a primarily Devotional Pathway) subscribe. But for the Hindu philosopher, the study of the Vedas is the supreme occupation and will lead one to Knowledge and to *moksa*, that is, release from bondage to karma and ignorance and attainment of peace within.

The Chinese culture spawned two great philosophical systems that are finding renewed interest in the West as we enter the twenty-first century. They are Confucianism, which is reflected in the great *Book of Changes* (the *I Ching*), and the philosophy of Laotzu, called the Tao, the Way. Although the philosophy of

Confucius greatly influenced the pattern of life adhered to in China, it was secular in nature. And the philosophy of Laotzu never developed into a religion in China. Only when it was merged with Buddhism in Japan, in the form of Zen Buddhism, did it cross over into the category of religion. Therefore, neither of these Chinese philosophies can properly be viewed as reflections of spiritual Pathways. In fact, China is perhaps the only great culture that has failed to give birth to its own tradition of spiritual Wisdom teachings.

No matter what one's religious tradition, it is possible to have access to the Path of Contemplation. However, the Buddhist and Hindu cultures offer a wider feast for the mind. It is perhaps for that reason that so many theoretical scientists in our time are turning to the East for their spiritual study.

# RELIGIONS
## and the Path of Self-Mastery

There is no religion that can properly be said to be a reflection of the Path of Self-Mastery. Although the putative founders of the world religions were no doubt all Self-realized and Masters of their own functioning, it is almost impossible for a group religion to develop around a Path that requires individualization. The individual achieves Self-Mastery through the diligent practice of disciplines. Although some of these disciplines can be taught in group settings, no group rituals, traditions, beliefs or doctrines can really be formulated as a basis for a group religion out of the disciplines of this Pathway.

In the East there is an ancient tradition that teaches the Path of Self-Mastery based on the Yoga philosophy that was first written down by Patanjali in the form of "Sutras," or aphorisms. But the practices based on those Sutras were passed on from teacher to student, from guru to disciple, and cannot properly be reduced to writing. Nor have they taken the form of a popular religion.

In the West there is also an ancient tradition that teaches the Path of Self-Mastery. It is best known as the Qabalah, the esoteric tradition of Judaism. The Qabalah incorporates teachings from Egypt and Greece that predate the formalizing of the Qabalistic method. Although the Qabalistic philosophy has been reduced to writing, the practices have not. They are properly taught only from teacher to student, as they have been for over two thousand years. (Fortune 5-6)

We do not, then, have examples within the great world religions of this Pathway. Both Judaism and Christianity have denounced the Path of Self-Mastery as white and black magic. What the religions term "magic," esoteric schools teach as formulae for mastering the forces of creation and in that way becoming co-creators. Until the end of the twentieth century when Western science began to experiment with genetic engineering, it was considered blasphemous for a Christian to aspire to co-creation. And within Judaism there was no less suspicion about the Qabalists who cast their spells and worked their magic.

Within Tibetan Buddhism there are many stories about yogis who developed powers to work with and transcend the forces of nature. However, most religious authorities would say that these stories are fables and not to be given credence, even though there is precedence for such feats in the practice of the Path of Self-Mastery.

Within most native religions the shaman, or medicine man/woman, the tribe's representative in the realm of Self-Mastery, walks this Pathway. The shaman stands in a line of succession and learns to handle powers of magic and healing under the close personal tutelage of another Master.

Scientists have long enjoyed making fun of the medieval alchemists, who worked with outer metals as symbols for the inner process of transformation they sought to bring to fulfillment in themselves. Alchemists were walking the Path of Self-Mastery.

Remnants of the Egyptian tradition of Self-Mastery have come down to us in the form of the Masonic Orders. However, these orders are not religions; they are fraternities of individuals who believe in the human capacity to transform human nature and to cooperate with the forces of nature. Individual Masons do not necessarily embody those beliefs, however.

The New Age movement is perhaps a step in the direction of preparing Westerners to step onto the Path of Self-Mastery. But the Self-Help Movement, important as it is, does not yet reach into the realm of spirit. It is limited to tinkering with the psyche from within the limited understandings of Western psychology.

Around the globe there are secret societies that have maintained the teachings of the earlier mystery and Wisdom schools, both East and West. When individuals are ready, from within whatever religious tradition, teachers are made known who can guide those individuals on the Path of Self-Mastery.

Again I would emphasize that religions are group expressions of rituals, practices and beliefs and cannot properly be called Pathways. Generally speaking, religions strongly discourage individuals from any direct experience that would serve as the basis for a challenge to ecclesiastical authority. Nevertheless, true seekers can penetrate the outer form of religion to the inner essence if they have eyes to see and ears to hear the larger Truth.

When your inner urge to pursue your own spiritual unfoldment with dedication and intensity becomes an inner pressure that you cannot resist, make your commitment to a Pathway and you will be led to the contacts you need to make your way. If you are part of a religious community, you may choose to remain within it for a time. Before long, however, if you follow the pattern of most treaders on Pathways, you will feel you no longer belong there. Then you will join the communion of all those who are walking Paths toward Union with all that is Lasting and True.

---

1. Matthew 13:10-16: "The disciples went up to him and asked, 'Why do you speak to them in parables?' He replied, 'It has been granted to you to know the secrets of the kingdom of Heaven; but to those others it has not been granted. . . . That is why I speak to them in parables; for they look without seeing, and listen without hearing or understanding. . . . But happy are your eyes because they see, and your ears because they hear!'"

2. A particularly fascinating account of this history is given by Alvin Boyd Kuhn in *Shadow of the Third Century,* Elizabeth, N.J.: Academy Press, 1949. It is available through the Theosophical Publishing House in Wheaton, Illinois. You can also find it on-line at http://www.geocities.com/Athens/Acropolis/2818/kuhn.html

3. Read Llewellyn Vaughan-Lee's *Sufism: The Transformation of the Heart*, Inverness, CA: The Golden Sufi Center, 1995 for a wonderful introduction to Sufism.

4. See Scholem, page 251.


**Works Cited:**
The New English Bible
Fortune, Dion. *The Mystical Qabalah.* York Beach, ME: Samuel
    Weiser, Inc., 2000.
Prabhavananda, Swami. *The Spiritual Heritage of India.*
    Hollywood: Vedanta Press, 1979.
Scholem, Gershom G. *Major Trends in Jewish Mysticism.* New
    York: Schoken Books, 1946.

# ALL IN ONE

*We may reach the same goal by different paths.*
— *Vivekananda*

Although we have used the metaphor of climbing a mountain to illustrate the nature of a spiritual Pathway, there is one all-important way the metaphor does not represent the true nature of spiritual development. The image of a mountain takes us outside of self, whereas all spiritual unfoldment occurs from within.

The outer metaphor serves because the vast majority of seekers live in an objective state of consciousness. They live as if the world is outside of them and they are moving through it. They live as if they are separate entities in a world of discrete objects, or things. Therefore, they can easily relate to the metaphor of a spiritual journey as analogous to climbing a mountain.

Let us conclude our consideration of Four Paths to Union, however, by acknowledging that in fact each of the Pathways represents an aspect of the growth of the individual self.

Imagine that you are in a deep sleep, unaware that you are a cell in the body of the One Self. From within that slumber of unconsciousness, you feel a stirring. Over time, you identify the stirring as a long-ing. You liken it to homesickness. It is a hollow feeling, as if a profound Love you once knew is no longer resident in you. You long to return to it, to reclaim it, to fill yourself with it again. You long to go Home.

To pursue that amorphous longing for something you once knew that satisfied your Heart is to step onto the Path of Devotion. It is to learn to love again, not as humans love, but as the Original One Loves: unconditionally and universally.

To develop the capacity to love universally is to bring forth one element of the Real Self's potential. You will return to this aspect of your growth again and again, in a cyclic fashion, until you are able to love perfectly according to the original pattern imprinted in your nature. Just as trees grow from season to season, each time becoming stronger and taller, so human beings develop over the course of many seasons. We call those seasons "lifetimes."

As you are learning to love unconditionally, you begin to develop awareness that more often than not you are motivated by urges and desires *other* than Love. This awareness causes you to observe yourself in order to learn why you do what you do and say what you say. The Path of Action represents this natural development of self-awareness regarding the inner urges that move you into outer action. And again, many seasons of growing and unfolding will occur before you have fully developed the capacity to make conscious choices about your motivations and your actions.

Noticing the contradictions in your own urges and motivations eventually awakens a curiosity about human nature. You begin to wonder what makes a human different from an animal and why human beings have self-awareness. Each question you ask will awaken further curiosity. Is there an Intelligence guiding the evolutionary process? Can we know that Intelligence? Is there an Ultimate Purpose and is there a purpose for your life? The Path of Contemplation represents the unfolding of your mental capacity to understand yourself and the world around you by asking questions and pursuing answers. Your understanding will expand as your experience of life grows through one cycle after another.

Your capacity for conscious and unconditional Love, conscious action, and conscious comprehension of the true nature of Reality will arouse an impatience within you to manifest more consistently what you know is possible. This is the fourth aspect of your growth, represented by the Path of Self-Mastery. To take more conscious responsibility for your self-expression, you focus on the faculty of will. Will is the alignment of your conscious self-awareness with a fundamental urge to become all that you are capable of being. Universal Will has been operating within you from the beginning, directing your development while you were unconscious and then awakening you from your deep sleep. You seek to consciously align with it so that you can become a co-creator of the next phases of your unfolding.

As the seasons of your lives multiply, you grow in wisdom and stature and become more and more conscious of who you are, why you are here, that you are integrally related to nature and other humans through a binding force called Love. You are a mirror-reflection of the Ultimate One and are therefore a co-creator in accordance with the Universal design.

You may cycle through these four Pathways, both

metaphorically and in disciplined practice, through many seasons of your spiritual growth in consciousness. Sometimes you will cycle through more than one Path in a lifetime. At other stages you may spend more than one lifetime on a given Pathway. You will not necessarily undertake the various aspects of your growth in the same order as they are presented here. You will focus on each according to your inner direction.

But eventually you will become fully developed in all four areas of your consciousness. In that way, all Four Pathways become One in your conscious, balanced and integrated Self-expression. At that stage of your unfolding you will live in a state of Union within, and your outer expression will be in total harmony with the larger Whole. You will live in peace and in power. You will be All in One and One with All.

# APPENDIX ONE:
# THE GATEWAY
# OF THE HEART

No matter which Pathway you choose to walk, you will eventually have to pass through a Gateway in order to reach the summit and experience the Union you desire. That Gateway is the opening of the Heart Center so that your capacity for unconditional Love can be realized.

The Heart Center is the balance point in the human energy system. It is the fulcrum that will make it possible for you to balance and integrate your inner spiritual life with your outer life of interaction in the world. Since Love is the binding force in the universe, it is inconceivable that you could experience Union with the Ultimate without opening the floodgates of your Heart to that Love which transcends human understanding.

If you walk the Path of Devotion, you will find the Gateway of the Heart at the entrance to the Path, for your life will be devoted to the embodiment of Love. On the Path of Action you will encounter the Gateway before you have traveled very far, for you cannot live a life of nonviolence without Love. On the Path of Self-Mastery you will quickly discover that without Love you cannot learn to cooperate with the laws that govern the universe and your own internal functions, for Love is the driving force that undergirds all those principles. It might be possible to walk the Path of Contemplation almost to the summit before passing through this Gateway, but if you are to merge with Absolute Truth, it will include unconditional Love.

As you prepare yourself to walk a Pathway, therefore, you will make your own way easier if you begin to cooperate with the opening of your Heart Center. **The Love Principles** are practical guidelines that will gradually open the floodgates and allow unconditional Love to flow through you.

**The Love Principles** were received and given expression by Arleen Lorrance in 1970 at a time when she committed herself to help transform the energy of despair and violence that permeated the ghetto high school where she was teaching. You can read that heart-warming story in her book called *The Love Project.*

Two other books that will introduce you to **The Love Principles** and help you to grasp how they are applied and lived in order to open the Gateway of the Heart are *The Love Principles,* also by Arleen Lorrance, and *The Love Project Way,* by Arleen Lorrance and Diane K. Pike.

**Works Cited**

Lorrance, Arleen. *The Love Principles.* Scottsdale, AZ: Teleos Imprint, 2001.

_____ *The Love Project.* San Diego: LP Publications, 1979.

_____ and Diane K. Pike. *The Love Project Way.* San Diego: LP Publications, 1980.

## THE LOVE PRINCIPLES

◆ Receive all people as beautiful
  exactly as they are.

◆ Have no expectations,
  but rather abundant expectancy.

◆ Provide others with opportunities to give.

◆ Problems are opportunities.

◆ Create your own reality consciously.

◆ Be the change you want to see happen
  instead of trying to change anyone else.

**Remember:** Choice is the life process.
  In every new moment of awareness,
  you can make a new choice.

You can begin right now to apply these principles in your life. You will soon discover the power of unconditional Love as it begins to transform you and the way you live in the world.

# APPENDIX TWO: EXPERIENCES OF UNION

To give you a taste of the joy that awaits you at the top of the mountain, here are some samples of personal experiences of union, at least one for each Pathway. You will notice how different each experience is from the others, partly due to the difference in the Pathways walked and partly due to the uniqueness of each individual.

## THE PATH OF DEVOTION

Thomas Raymond Kelly was born on June 4, 1893 on a farm in southwestern Ohio to parents who were ardent Quakers. In the first 44 years of his life, he walked the Path of Contemplation, fervently pursuing philosophy as a search for Truth in which both his religious hunger and his passion for science might be fulfilled. But in 1937 he shifted to the Path of Devotion. He retained his respect for science, scholarship and method, but it fell into a secondary place, for he had been, as he put it, "literally melted down by the love of God." Here are words from his *Testament of Devotion* describing the summit as he experienced it walking the Pathway of Devotion, but framing his description as questions for the reader to ponder:

Let me talk very intimately and very earnestly with you about Him who is dearer than life. Do you really want to live your lives, every moment of your lives, in His Presence? Does every drop of blood in your body love Him? Does every breath you draw breathe a prayer, a praise to Him? Do you sing and dance within yourselves, as you glory in His love? Have you set yourselves to be His, and only His, walking every moment in holy obedience? I know I'm talking like an old-time evangelist. But I can't help that, nor dare I restrain myself and get prim and conventional. We have too long been prim and restrained. The fires of the love of God, of our love toward God, and of His love toward us, are very hot. "Thou shalt love the Lord thy God with all thy heart and soul and mind and strength." Do we really do it? Is love steadfastly directed toward God, in our minds, all day long? Do we intersperse our work with gentle prayers and praises to Him? Do we live in the steady peace of God, a peace down at the very depths of our souls, where all strain is gone and God is already victor over the world, already victor over our weaknesses? This life, this abiding, enduring peace that never fails, this serene power and unhurried conquest, inward conquest over ourselves, outward conquest over the world, is meant to be ours. It is a life that is freed from strain and anxiety and hurry, for something of the Cosmic Patience of God becomes ours. Are our lives unshakable, because we are clear down on bedrock, rooted and grounded in the love of God? This is the first and the great commandment.

There is a way of life so hid with Christ in God that in the midst of the day's business one is inwardly lifting brief prayers, short ejaculations of praise, subdued whispers of adoration and of tender love to the Beyond that is within . . . Now out from such a holy Center come the commissions of life. Our fellowship with God issues in world-concern. (Pages 119-120)

Here is the same realization of the highest Ideal of Perfect Love, expressed in the words of another great Bhakti-Yogi (one who walks the Path of Devotion), Keshub Chander Sen, who lived in Bengal, India, in the first half of this century:

> All is tranquil and hushed within. Only a sense of self fills the soul. The devotee calls out to it to disappear. And it vanishes away. Then the Infinite bursts upon his view. He shines as something tremendously real — a burning reality. From the depths of his being this Presence surges up as the fountain of reality. From above it descends like a continual shower of inspiration. From all sides it draws near as the presence of one who is nearest and dearest. And the deeper the insight the brighter the illumination and the sweeter the Presence. The mere Presence is soon transformed into a Person with Intelligence, Love and Holiness. As the union ripens and develops the spirit-bonds become lighter and more and more of the Infinite is drawn into the finite soul. Gradually the Almighty overpowers, captivates and entrances the devotee's little soul. Father and Mother, Friend and Guide, Teacher and Savior, Comforter and Gladdener are all combined in this one Person. If there is any such thing as a spiritual smile it plays on His lips. (Younghusband 53)

In our Western religions, we are accustomed to hearing God, the Infinite, referred to as "He," but in the East there are many who experience union with the Mother-God. Here, in the words of Ramakrishna, one of the greatest Indian Bhakti-Yogis of this century, is just such an account:

Suddenly the blessed Mother revealed herself to me . . . The buildings with their different parts, the temple and all vanished from my sight, leaving no trace whatever. In their stead was a limitless, infinite, effulgent ocean of Spirit. As far as the eye could reach, its shining billows were madly rushing towards me with a terrific noise. In the twinkling of an eye they were on me. I was completely engulfed . . . and I fell unconscious on the floor. What happened externally after that I do not know. But within me there was a steady flow of undiluted bliss, altogether new. I was feeling the presence of the Divine Mother. (Younghusband 65-66)

## THE PATH OF ACTION

I referred often to Mohandas K. Gandhi in the chapter on this Pathway, but it is worth quoting him again here. In his autobiography, which he subtitled *The Story of My Experiments with Truth*, Gandhi revealed his glimpses of the mountain top in bits and pieces. I offer one example. After telling about an experience in civil resistance when he went to help the peasants of Champaran, he wrote:

The people had for the moment lost all fear of punishment and yielded obedience to the power of love which their new friend exercised . . . No political work had yet been done amongst them. The world outside Champaran was not known to them. And yet they received me as though we had been age-long friends. It is no exaggeration, but the literal truth, to say that in this meeting with the peasants I was face to face with God, Ahimsa [nonviolence] and Truth.

When I come to examine my title to this realization, I find nothing but my love for the people. And this in turn is nothing but an expression of my unshakable faith in Ahimsa. (411-412)

To see God in the people he was serving is certainly the experience of Union for one walking the Path of Action. At the end of his autobiography, Gandhi states in summary fashion what he had learned from walking his Pathway up to that point. He writes:

My uniform experience has convinced me that there is no other God than Truth. And . . . the only means for the realization of Truth is Ahimsa . . . However sincere my strivings after Ahimsa may have been, they have still been imperfect and inadequate. The little fleeting glimpses, therefore, that I have been able to have of Truth can hardly convey an idea of the indescribable luster of Truth, a million times more intense than that of the sun we daily see with our eyes. In fact what I have caught is only the faintest glimmer of that mighty effulgence. But this much I can say with assurance, as a result of all my experiments, that a perfect vision of Truth can only follow a complete realization of Ahimsa.

To see the universal and all-pervading Spirit of truth face to face one must be able to love the meanest of creation as oneself. And a man who aspires after that cannot afford to keep out of any field of life. That is why my devotion to Truth has drawn me into the field of politics; and I can say without the slightest hesitation, and yet in all humility, that those who say that religion has nothing to do with politics do not know what religion means.

. . . The experiences and experiments have sustained me and given me great joy. But I know that I have still before me a difficult Path to traverse. I must reduce myself to zero. So long as a man does not of his own free will put himself last among his fellow creatures, there is no salvation for him. Ahimsa is the farthest limit of humility. (503-505)

Gandhi's autobiography was finished in 1929. From the time he wrote the above closing words to his death in 1948 he certainly walked a long way toward the perfection of humility in his own expression of nonviolence, so that as he died at the hand of an assassin, he breathed out a blessing to the man that killed him.

Abdul Ghaffar Khan (1890-1988) was a devout Muslim and a devoted ally of Mahatma Gandhi's in the struggle for nonviolence. Badshah Kahn, as he was known (which means "king of khans"), was often called the Frontier Gandhi because he, of all Gandhi's followers, best mirrored the fullness of Gandhi's way. He raised an army of one hundred thousand nonviolent soldiers out of one of the world's most violent peoples, the Pathans. The Pathans are an ethnic tribe of Muslims who live on the border between Pakistan and India.

We do not have this account of his mountain top experience in his own words, but in *Nonviolent Soldier of Islam,* Eknath Easwaran writes of the fast Khan performed when he was twenty-three:

> Kahn stayed in a small, dim room for several days, eating nothing. At night he sipped creek water. And he prayed. When his knees tired of kneeling, he sat cross-legged on the prayer carpet.
>
> He sought answers ... What should he do? ... to judge from his own terse references, his chilla (fast) in the mosque at Zagai was clouded and inconclusive. But it can be observed from that point on that his activities and words are stamped with a singleness of purpose – the

service of God – that does not alter over the course of eight decades . . .

It was early morning when Ghaffar Khan ended his fast. He folded his prayer rug under his arm and walked out with the vague but powerful awareness that he was not the same man who had entered the mosque a few days before. He had not received the direct answers he had sought – he still did not know what to do. But he felt a strength he had not known before. And he understood, dimly, that it was the strength of God.

*Islam!* Inside him, the word began to explode with meaning. *Islam!* [which means] Submit! Surrender to the Lord and know His strength! Ghaffar felt swelling within him the desire to serve this great God. And since He needed no service, Ghaffar would serve His creatures instead – the tattered villagers who were too ignorant and too steeped in violence to help themselves . . .

He saw before him only pain and unending labor. But he felt buoyed . . . He did not fully understand the nature of his calling; but he knew he had been called. He would submit and he would not seek rest in this life. (70-71)

This was the confirmation of his calling to walk the Path of Action, which he did, faithfully, for over eighty years.

## THE PATH OF CONTEMPLATION

Franklin Merrell-Wolff was born in California toward the end of the nineteenth century. He was the son of a Christian clergyman and was trained in mathematics, physics and philosophy on three continents. His awakening to knowledge through union with it — what he calls "Knowledge through Identity"— came in

August of 1936. It is an example of union experienced by one walking on the Path of Contemplation:

I had been sitting in a porch swing, reading . . . I turned to the section devoted to "Liberation," as I seemed to feel an especial hunger for this. I covered the material quickly and it all seemed very clear and satisfactory. Then, as I sat afterward dwelling in thought upon the subject just read, suddenly it dawned upon me that a common mistake made in the higher meditation—i.e., meditation for Liberation—is the seeking for a subtle object of Recognition, in other words, something that could be experienced. Of course, I had long known the falseness of this position theoretically, yet failed to recognize it. (Here is a subtle but very important distinction.) At once, I dropped expectation of having anything happen. Then with eyes open and no sense stopped in functioning—hence no trance—I abstracted the subjective moment—the "I AM" or "Atman" element—from the totality of the objective consciousness manifold. Upon this I focused. Naturally, I found what, from the relative point of view, is Darkness and Emptiness. But I Realized It as Absolute Light and Fullness and that I was That. Of course, I cannot tell what IT was in Its own nature. The relative forms of consciousness inevitably distort nonrelative Consciousness. Not only can I not tell this to others, I cannot even contain it within my own relative consciousness, whether of sensation, feeling, or thought. Every metaphysical thinker will see this impossibility at once. I was even prepared not to have the personal consciousness share in this Recognition in any way. But in this I was happily disappointed.

Presently I felt the Ambrosia-quality in the breath with the purifying benediction that it casts over the whole personality, even including the physical body. I found myself above the universe, not in the sense of leaving the physical body and being taken out in space, but in the sense of being above space, time, and causality. My karma seemed to drop away from me as an individual responsibility. I felt intangibly, yet wonderfully, free. I sustained this universe and was not bound by it. Desires and ambitions grew perceptibly more and more shadowy. All Worldly honors were without power to exalt me. Physical life seemed undesirable. Repeatedly, through the days that followed, I was in a state of deep brooding, thinking thoughts that were so abstract that there were no concepts to represent them. I seemed to comprehend a veritable library of Knowledge, all less concrete than the most abstract mathematics. The personality rested in a gentle glow of happiness, but while it was very gentle, yet it was so potent as to dull the keenest sensuous delight. Likewise the sense of world-pain was absorbed. I looked, as it were, over the world asking: "What is there of interest here? What is there worth doing?" I found but one interest: the desire that other souls should also realize this that I had realized, for in it lay the one effective key for the solving of their problems. The little tragedies of men left me indifferent. I saw one great Tragedy, the cause of all the rest, the failure of man to realize his own Divinity. I saw but one solution, The Realization of this Divinity. (4-5)

The abstract description Franklin-Merrell gives of his experience is typical of one walking the Path of Contemplation. I have written about Krishnamurti as an exemplar in the chapter on this Pathway. Here is his description, given in his notebook, of one of his mountain top experiences. It is equally abstract.

The room became full of that benediction. Now what followed is almost impossible to put down in words; words are such dead things, with definite set meanings and what took place was beyond all words and description. It was the center of all creation; it was a purifying seriousness that cleansed the brain of every thought, and feeling; its seriousness was as lightning which destroys and burns up; the profundity of it was not measurable, it was there immovable, impenetrable, a solidity that was as light as the heavens. It was in the eye, in the breath. It was in the eyes and the eyes could see. The eyes that saw, that looked were wholly different from the eyes of the organ and yet they were the same eyes. There was only seeing, the eyes that saw beyond time-space. There was impenetrable dignity and a peace that was the essence of all movement, action. No virtue touched it for it was beyond all virtue and sanctions of man. There was love that was utterly perishable and so it had the delicacy of all new things, vulnerable, destructible and yet it was beyond all this. It was there imperishable, unnameable, the unknowing. No thought could ever touch it. It was "pure," untouched so ever dyingly beautiful.

All this seemed to affect the brain; it was not as it was before. (Thought is such a trivial thing, necessary but trivial.) Because of it, relationship seems to have changed. As a terrific storm, a destructive earthquake gives a new course to the rivers, changes the landscape, digs deep into the earth, so it has leveled the contours of thought, changed the shape of the heart. (Lutyens, 113)

## THE PATH OF SELF-MASTERY

Gopi Krishna (1903-1984) was born in the small village of Gairoon, about 20 miles from Srinagar, the capital of Kashmir, of a family of hard-working and God-fearing peasants. He began the practice of meditation at the age of seventeen, motivated by his failure in a house examination at the College, which prevented him from appearing in the University that year. He realized that by his lack of self-control he had betrayed the trust his mother had placed in him and he did not want to be guilty of the same offence again. He knew that to regulate his conduct he needed to conquer his mind and he began to read books to find out how he could accomplish that. He culled from a huge mass of material two things: concentration of mind and cultivation of will, two things that characterize the Path of Self-mastery. Seventeen years later, at age 34, he had the following experience of the mountain top, as described in his book *Kundalini: The Evolutionary Energy in Man*:

> One morning during the Christmas of 1937 I sat cross-legged in a small room in a little house on the outskirts of the town of Jammu, the winter capital of the Jammu and Kashmir State in northern India. I was meditating with my face towards the window on the east through which the first grey streaks of the slowly brightening dawn fell into the room. Long practice had accustomed me to sit in the same posture for hours at a time without the least discomfort, and I sat breathing slowly and rhythmically, my attention drawn towards the crown of my head, contemplating an imaginary lotus in full bloom, radiating light.
>
> I sat steadily, unmoving and erect, my thoughts uninterruptedly centered on the shining lotus, intent on keeping my attention from wandering and bringing it back again and again whenever it moved in any other direction. The intensity of concentration interrupted my breathing; gradually it slowed down to such an extent that at times it was barely perceptible. My whole being was so engrossed in the contemplation of the lotus that for several minutes at a time I lost touch with my body and surroundings. During such intervals I used to feel as if I were poised in mid-air, without any feeling of a body around me. The only object of which I was aware was a lo-

tus of brilliant colour, emitting rays of light. This experience has happened to many people who practise meditation in any form regularly for a sufficient length of time, but what followed on that fateful morning in my case, changing the whole course of my life and outlook, has happened to few.

During one such spell of intense concentration I suddenly felt a strange sensation below the base of the spine, at the place touching the seat, while I sat cross-legged on a folded blanket spread on the floor. The sensation was so extraordinary and so pleasing that my attention was forcibly drawn towards it. The moment my attention was thus unexpectedly withdrawn from the point on which it was focused, the sensation ceased. Thinking it to be a trick played by my imagination to relax the tension, I dismissed the matter from my mind and brought my attention back to the point from which it had wandered. Again I fixed it on the lotus, and as the image grew clear and distinct at the top of my head, again the sensation occurred. This time I tried to maintain the fixity of my attention and succeeded for a few seconds, but the sensation extending upwards grew so intense and was so extraordinary, as compared to anything I had experienced before, that in spite of myself my mind went towards it, and at that very moment it again disappeared. I was now convinced that something unusual had happened for which my daily practice of concentration was probably responsible.

I had read glowing accounts, written by learned men, of great benefits resulting from concentration, and of the miraculous powers acquired by yogis through such exercises. My heart began to beat wildly, and I found it difficult to bring my attention to the required degree of fixity. After a while I grew composed and was soon as deep in meditation as before. When completely immersed I again experienced the sensation, but this time, instead of allowing my mind to leave the point where I had fixed it, I maintained a rigidity of attention throughout. The sensation again extended upwards, growing in intensity, and I felt myself wavering; but with a great effort I kept my attention centered round the lotus. Suddenly, with a roar like that of a waterfall, I felt a stream of liquid light entering my brain through the spinal cord.

Entirely unprepared for such a development, I was completely taken by surprise; but regaining self-control instantaneously, I remained sitting in the same posture, keeping my mind on the point of concentration. The illumination grew brighter and brighter, the roaring louder, I experienced a rocking sensation and then felt myself slipping out of my body, entirely enveloped in a halo of light. It is impossible to describe the experience accurately. I felt the point of consciousness that was myself growing wider, surrounded by waves of light. It grew wider and wider, spreading outward while the body, normally the immediate object of its perception, appeared to have receded into the distance until I became entirely unconscious of it. I was now all consciousness, without any outline, without any idea of a corporeal appendage, without any feeling or sensation coming from the senses, immersed in a sea of light simultaneously conscious and aware of every point, spread out, as it were, in all directions without any barrier or material obstruction. I was no longer myself, or to be more accurate, no longer as I knew myself to be, a small point of awareness confined in a body, but instead was a vast circle of consciousness in which the body was but a point, bathed in light and in a state of exaltation and happiness impossible to describe. (11-13)

You will notice how explicit the details of the experience *in the body* are in Gopi Krishna's account. This is reflective of the Path of Self-Mastery. He sought to know how to control and direct his own forces and his self-observation was essential to that task.

With these examples in your consciousness, you will easily be able to identify other mountain top experiences as you read about them or hear others describe them. The descriptions will vary, but the quality of the events will be very similar. Moreover, you will begin to identify the effects on people's lives of knowing Union.

When the time comes for your own direct experience, you will enter into the fellowship of those who have experienced Union. Your consciousness will be transformed to such an extent that you will never see or understand things quite the same way again. Although the process of transformation in your personality, and the further expansion of your consciousness, will continue, the experience of Union will never leave you.

## Works Cited

Easwaran, Eknath. *Nonviolent Soldier of Islam: Badshah Khan, A Man to Match His Mountains.* Tomales, CA: Nilgiri Press, 1999.

Gandhi, Mohandas K. *An Autobiography: The Story of My Experiments with Truth.* Boston: Beacon Press, 1957.

Kelly, Thomas R. *A Testament of Devotion.* New York: Harper and Brothers, 1941.

Krishna, Gopi. *Kundalini: The Evolutionary Energy in Man.* Berkeley, CA: Shambala, 1971.

Lutyens, Mary. *Krishnamurti: The Years of Fulfillment.* New York: Farrar, Straus, Giroux, 1983.

Merrell-Wolff, Franklin. *Pathways through to Space.* New York: The Julian Press, 1983.

Younghusband, Sir Francis. *Modern Mystics.* New York: Books for Libraries Press, Inc., 1967.

# APPENDIX THREE:
# SUGGESTED READINGS

The following is not intended to be a comprehensive bibliography. Instead, it is meant to provide you with some places to start if you want to read further about one or more of the Pathways presented in this book.

## General Readings

Lorrance, Arleen. *The Love Principles.* Scottsdale, AZ: Teleos Imprint, 2001.

─────────── and Diane K. Pike. *The Love Project Way.* San Diego: LP Publications, 1980.
> Since the doorway to the spiritual life is through the Heart, either of these books on *The Love Principles* will provide you will tools to aid you as you prepare to step onto a spiritual Pathway.

Prabhavananda, Swami. *The Spiritual Heritage of India,* Hollywood: Vedanta Press, 1979. Foreword by Huston Smith.
> An excellent introduction to the rich tradition of spiritual wisdom that has been cultivated and preserved in India for five or six thousand years.

Vivekananda, Swami. *The Complete Works of Vivekananda.* Hollywood: Vedanta Press, 1947.

*Vivekananda is widely recognized as one of the
authorities on Yogic philosophy and the Four Pathways.*

## Further reading for the Path of Devotion:

*Books by or about any of the following exemplars of
this Pathway will serve you:* Rumi, Ramakrishna, Sai
Baba, St. Frances of Assisi, The Little Flower, Ananda
Moyma, the Baal Shem Tov.

Brother Lawrence. *The Practice of the Presence of God.*
Westwood, NJ: Fleming H. Revell Co., 1958.

Kelly, Thomas R. *A Testament of Devotion.* New York:
Harper and Brothers, 1941.

Keyes, Laurel Elizabeth. *Sundial: I Count the Sunny Hours.*
Denver: Gentle Living Publications, 1979.

Moss, Richard M.D. *The I That Is We.* Millbrae, CA: Celes-
tial Arts, 1981.

Nicholson, Reynold A. *Studies in Islamic Mysticism.* Cambridge: Cambridge University Press, 1967.

Smith, Margaret. *Rabia The Mystic and Her Fellow-Saints
in Islam.* Cambridge: Cambridge University Press,
1928.

St. John of the Cross, The Works of.

St. John's Gospel

St. Teresa of Avila, The Works of.

Teresa of Calcutta, Mother. *My Life for the Poor,* edited by
Jose Luis Bonzalez-Balado and Janet N. Playfoot. San
Francisco: Harper & Row, 1985.

*Other works by and about Mother Teresa will give you a wonderful feeling for what it is to walk this Pathway.*

Vaughan-Lee, Llewellyn. *Sufism: The Transformation of the Heart.* Inverness, CA: The Golden Sufi Center, 1995.
*A fresh and clear guide to walking the Path of Devotion.*

Vivekananda, Swami. *Bhakti-Yoga: The Yoga of Love and Devotion.* Hollywood: Vedanta Press, 1978. (Also available from the Ramakrishna Vivekananda Center in New York.)
*This is a definitive description of the Path of Devotion.*

Younghusband, Sir Francis. *Modern Mystics.* New York: Books for Libraries Press, Inc., 1967.

## Further Reading for the Path of Action:

*Books by or about any of the following exemplars of this Pathway will serve you:* Albert Schweitzer, Martin Luther King, Jr., Clara Barton, Eleanor Roosevelt, Nelson Mandela, Cesar Chavez, Dorothy Day, and Susan B. Anthony.

Black, Jo Anne, Nick Harvey, and Laurel Robertson. *Gandhi the Man.* San Francisco: Glide Publications, 1972.

Easwaran, Eknath. *Nonviolent Soldier of Islam: Badshah Khan, A Man to Match His Mountains.* Tomales, CA: Nilgiri Press, 1999.

Esposito, John L. *Islam: The Straight Path.* New York/Oxford: Oxford University Press, 1988.

Gandhi, Mohandas K. *An Autobiography: The Story of My Experiments with Truth.* Boston: Beacon Press, 1957.
*There is no more outstanding and inspiring example of the Path of Action than Gandhi.*

Laotzu. *The Way of Life,* an American version by Witter Bynner. New York: The John Day Company, 1944.

Lippman, Thomas W. *Understanding Islam: An Introduction to the Moslem World.* New York: New American Library, 1982.

Lorrance, Arleen. *The Love Project.* San Diego: LP Publications, 1972.

Vivekananda, Swami. *Karma-Yoga.* Hollywood: Vedanta Press, 1999.

## Further Reading for the Path of Contemplation:

*Books by or about any of the following exemplars of this Pathway will serve you:* Samkara, Sri Aurobindo, Plato, Maimonides, Krishnamurti, Nisargadatta.

Arnold, Sir Edwin. *The Light of Asia or The Great Renunciation.* Wheaton, IL: The Theosophical Publishing House, 1971.

Aurobindo, Sri. *The Mind of Light.* New York: E. P. Dutton & Co., 1971.
    *Sri Aurobindo was an exemplar of this Pathway. Any of his works are worth reading to give you insight into the mind of one who walks the Path of Contemplation.*

Buber, Martin. *I and Thou.* New York: Charles Scribner's Sons, 1958.

Krishnamurti, Jiddu. *Freedom from the Known,* San Francisco: Harper San Francisco, 1975, *and any of the other many books written by Krishnamurti.*

Lutyens, Mary. *Krishnamurti: The Years of Awakening.* New York: Farrar, Straus, Giroux, 1975.
_____ *Krishnamurti: The Years of Fulfillment.* New York: Farrar, Straus, Giroux, 1983.

Merrell-Wolff, Franklin. *Pathways through to Space* and *The Philosophy of Consciousness without an Object.* New York: The Julian Press, 1983.

Nisargadatta Maharaj. *I Am That.* Durham, NC: Acorn Press, 1973.

*The Teachings of the Compassionate Buddha*, edited, with commentary, by E. A. Burtt. New York: Mentor Books, 1963.

Vivekananda, Swami. *Jnana-Yoga.* Hollywood: Vedanta Press, 1982.
A definitive presentation of the Path of Contemplation.

## Further Reading for the Path of Self-Mastery:

*Books by or about any of the following exemplars of this Pathway will serve you:* Yogananda, Vivekananda, Vitvan, The Mother (Mirra Alfassa), Madame Blavatsky, Dion Fortune, Ouspensky, Gurdjieff, J. G. Bennett.

Fortune, Dion. *The Mystical Qabalah.* York Beach, ME: Samuel Weiser, Inc., 2000.
*Dion Fortune has written many books that will serve you in your quest to understand or walk this Pathway.*

Gurdjieff, G. I. *Life Is Real Only Then, When 'I Am.'* New York: Viking Arkana, 1991.

> *Gurdjieff is an exemplar of this Pathway and any of his own books will enlighten you further about the Path of Self-Mastery.*

Krishna, Gopi. *Kundalini: The Evolutionary Energy in Man.* Berkeley, CA: Shambala, 1971.
> *Any of Gopi Krishna's books serve as excellent examples of the Path of Self-Mastery.*

*Mother's Agenda 1951-1973.* Volumes 1 through 13. New York: Institute for Evolutionary Research, 1979.
> *The Mother, of Sri Aurobindo's ashram, embodied the Path of Self-Mastery. Her agendas, and distillations from them, will be an inspiration to you if you choose to walk this Pathway.*

Ouspensky, P.D. *The Fourth Way.* New York: Vintage Books, 1971.
> *This is an excellent introduction to Gurdjieff, an exemplar of this Pathway. Any of his own books or others books by Ouspensky and other disciples of Gurdjieff's will enlighten you further about the Path of Self-Mastery.*

Patanjali's *Yoga Aphorisms.*

Satprem. *The Mind of the Cells, or Willed Mutation of Our Species.* New York: Institute for Evolutionary Research, 1982.
_____. *Life without Death.* New York: Institute for Evolutionary Research, 1988.
> *These two books by Satprem reflect on The Mother's contribution to Self-Mastery.*

Satriano, Richard. *Vitvan: An American Master.* Baker, NV: School of the Natural Order, 1977.

Vitvan. *The Christos.* Baker, NV: School of the Natural Order, 1979.

_____. *Self-Mastery through Meditation.* Baker, NV: School of the Natural Order, 1982.
> *Any of Vitvan's books and class series present this Pathway with an emphasis on correlating it with modern physics and the science of General Semantics.*

Vivekananda, Swami. *Raja-Yoga.* Hollywood: Vedanta Press, 1953.
> *Vivekananda is considered an expert on this Pathway and his presentation of it is definitive.*

Yogananda, Paramahansa. *Autobiography of a Yogi.* Los Angeles: Self-Realization Fellowship, 1969.